Samsung Watch Guide

The Comprehensive Step-by-Step and Illustrated Manual for Beginners and Seniors to Master the Samsung Galaxy Watch 6 with Tips and Tricks

Shawn Blaine

Copyright © 2023 by Shawn Blaine - All rights reserved.

This book is copyrighted, and no part may be reproduced, or transmitted via any means, be it electronic, internet, mechanical, or otherwise without the consent of the publisher except in a brief quotation or review of the book.

Table of Contents

Introduction 1

Chapter One 3

Set up Samsung Galaxy Watch 3

Turn on Watch 8

Charge the Galaxy Watch 8

Charge with Wireless PowerShare 9

Back up Galaxy Watch 11

Reset your Galaxy Watch 14

Enable Mobile Networks 16

Chapter Two 18

Change Brightness 18

Change Screen Timeout 19

Enable Always on Display 20

Clear Storage 20

Change the Wrist Orientation 21

Enable Bluetooth 22

Enable Disconnection Alerts 22

Enable Wi-Fi 23

Pair Bluetooth Headphones with Watch 23

Enable Airplane Mode 25

Enable Power Saving Mode 26

Add Screen Lock 28

Chapter Three 29

Adjust the Watch's Face 29

Personalize the Watch Face 32

Add your Photo as Watch Face 37

Chapter Four 41

Setting up Bixby 41

Enable Voice Commands 41

Setting up Google Assistant 42

Enable Google Assistant............................... 44

Adjust the Home Key Settings 47

Chapter Five 50

Change when to Show Alerts......................... 50

Select Apps that can Send Alerts................... 52

Enable Water Lock 53

Enable Bedtime Mode 56

Enable Theater Mode 58

Enable Do Not Disturb 59

Change the Voice Assistant's Language 60

Change the Voice Input Language 61

Change the Keyboard Input Language 62

Set the Time and Date 63

Chapter Six 65

Install Apps on your Watch........................... 65

Uninstall Apps 67

Manage Apps Data 68

Update your Watch Software 74

Update Watch Apps 75
How to Use Google Maps 76
Using the Camera Controller 79
Using the Gallery App 79
Chapter Seven 81
Personalize Visibility Enhancements 81
Turn on TalkBack 81
Customize Hearing 82
Enable Accessibility Shortcut 83
Enable Double Press Key 83
Chapter Eight 85
Set up Samsung Pay 85
Enable NFC 89
Add an Alarm 90
Mute/Snooze an Alarm 90
Remove an Alarm 91
Use Stopwatch 91
Add a Timer 92
Stop the Timer 92
Chapter Nine 93
Set up Workout 93
Enable Continuous Heart Rate 94
   Measure Heart Rate Manually 94
   Get High or Low Heart Rate Alert 95
Enable Automatic Workout Detection 95

Enable Snore Detection 96
Enable Sleep Coaching 97
Quit Sleep Coaching 98
Enable Fall Detection 98
Measure Stress 99
Track your Steps 100
Monitor Woman's Health 103
Track your Body Composition 107
Disable Coaching Messages 110
Measure ECG 111
Measure Blood Pressure 114
Measure your SpO2 115
    Adding the Blood Oxygen Tile 116
    Track Blood Oxygen 116
    Enable Blood Oxygen Tracking during Sleep 116
Track Floors Count 117
Track Caffeine Intake 117
Chapter Ten 119
Make and Answer Calls 119
Answer Calls 120
Sending a Text Message 120
How to use Quick Messages 121
Remove Messages 121
Block Message Alerts 122
Block Messages 122

Enable SOS 123
Chapter Eleven 124
Use the Samsung Flow App 124
    Connecting Devices via Bluetooth 124
    Unlock the Computer/Tablet 125
    Unlock your Computer/Tablet with Simple Unlock 125
Manage PowerPoint Presentations with Watch 126
    Manage the Slides 126
    Enable Presentation Alerts 127
Chapter Twelve 129
Import Music to the Watch 129
Remove Imported Music 129
Set up Vibration 130
Enable Call Vibration 130
Notification Vibration 131
Set Watch Volume 131
Add Ringtone 132
Add Notification Sound 132
Conclusion 133
About the Author 134
Other Books by the Author 135
Index 136

Introduction

The Galaxy Watch 6 features 40mm and 44mm variants with 1.3-inch and 1.5-inch Super AMOLED displays, respectively. They all come with an always-on Display. Samsung has added an improved processor with the addition of the Exynos W930 SoC.

The smartwatch now offers thinner bezels and has a larger active display area than the previous model. However, it doesn't feature the rotating crown like the Classic version. Samsung has added the One UI 5 Watch to this model, which is a new version based on Wear OS 4.

You can track your sleeping habits and view a comprehensive chart of your sleeping history, and these can be used to suggest the best sleeping advice and recommendations. This is enabled by a feature called "Sleep Coaching."

Other great features of the Galaxy Watch 6 include an irregular heart rhythm alert, which was also in the previous model.

Your smartwatch can automatically detect when you're cycling, swimming, or running. Another feature that still makes it is fall detection, which sends an alert to your emergency contacts whenever you have a hard fall. Guess what? The smartwatch is able to track basal body temperature at bedtime, which is useful for monitoring menstrual cycles.

Unlike the previous model, if you wish to pair your smartwatch with a new smartphone, you won't require a full reset thanks to improvements in Wear OS 4.

With Gesture controls, you're able to control and alternate between the different camera modes on the paired smartphone directly from your Galaxy Watch.

The smartwatch also boasts 2 GB of RAM and 16GB of storage capacity.

This user guide has been written to help you operate and master your Samsung Galaxy Watch 6 like a pro. This guide provides an easy-to-follow outline with pictorial illustrations to explain each concept and setup guide, thereby saving you time and effort. With this manual, you'll be able to set up and operate the Samsung Galaxy Watch 6 all by yourself without assistance.

This is the book to get you started, whether you're a senior or a beginner; if you're an expert, it will become your go-to reference.

Chapter One

Set up Samsung Galaxy Watch

- Ensure you've charged the smartwatch fully before powering it up for the first time.
- Long-tap the home key on the smartwatch to power it on.
- On your smartphone, head to the App Store to download the Galaxy Wearable app.

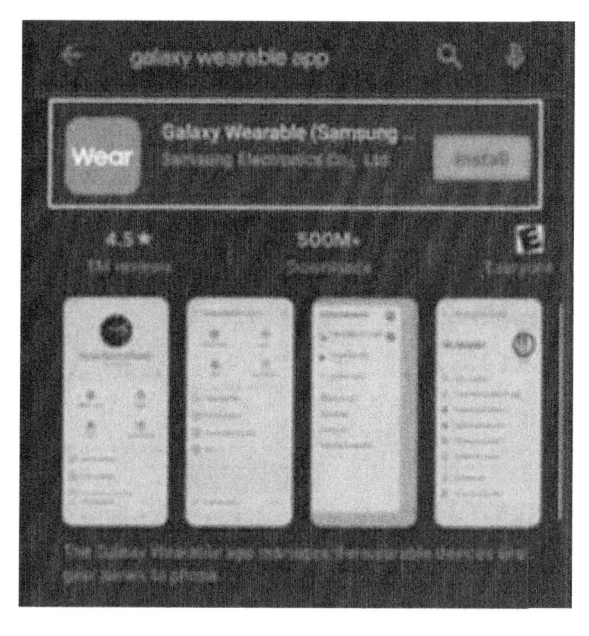

- Once you're done installing the Galaxy Wearable app on your smartphone, open it. Then press "**Start**."

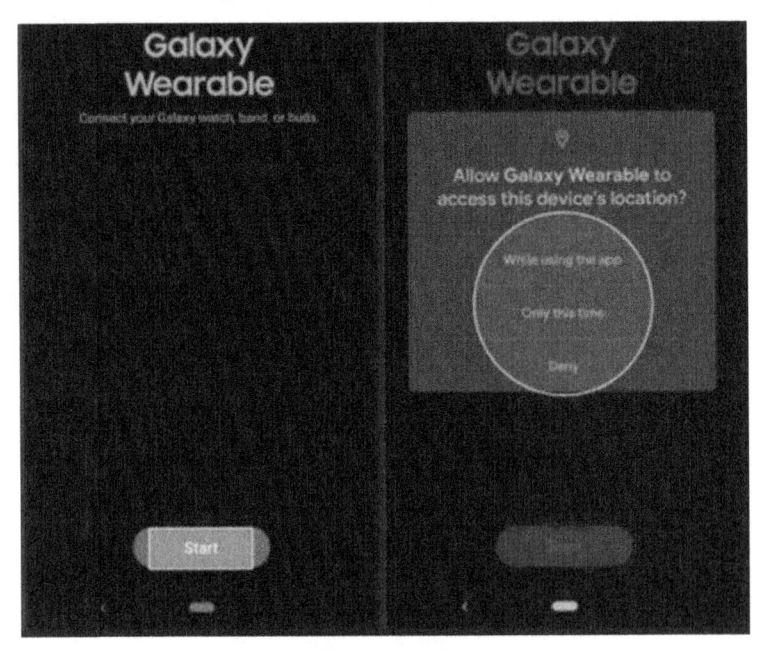

- On the menu requesting location access, choose any of the desired options: "**Deny**," "**Only this time**," or "**While using the app**."
- From the next interface, press "**Allow**" so that your Galaxy Watch can manage phone calls.

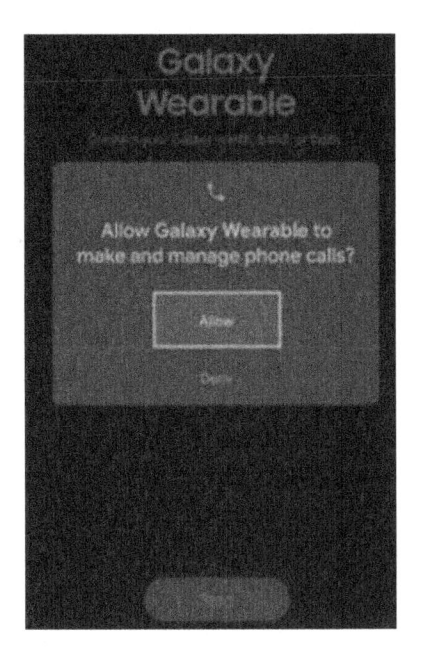

- Now, press "**Galaxy Watch6**" the moment it pops up on the list of available devices.
- On the next interface, compare the code on your Galaxy Watch and that on your smartphone to ensure they're the same, then choose "**Pair**."
- Check the radio button to authorize contact access and call logs on your smartwatch.
- Now, press "**OK**."

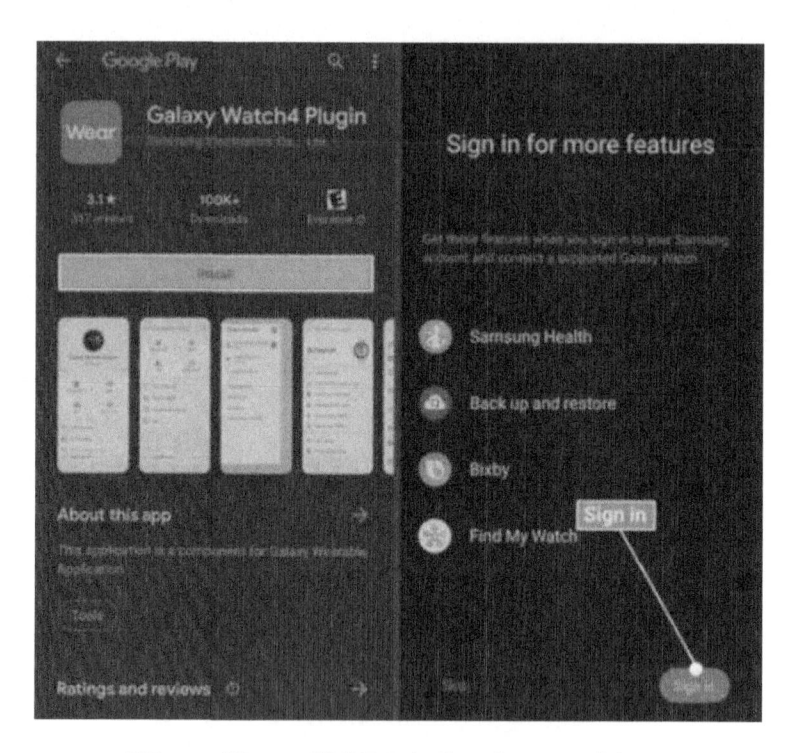

- Hit on "**Install**." Wait for the watch's plugin to install on your smartphone.
- Then, choose "**Sign in**."
- After filling in your Samsung login data, choose "**Sign in**."

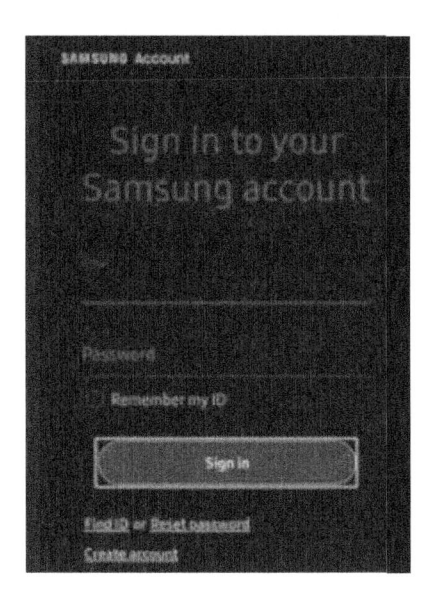

- Hit on "**Create account**" if you're yet to create a Samsung account. However, if you have one already, choose "**Continue**."
- Go through the onscreen prompts to proceed.

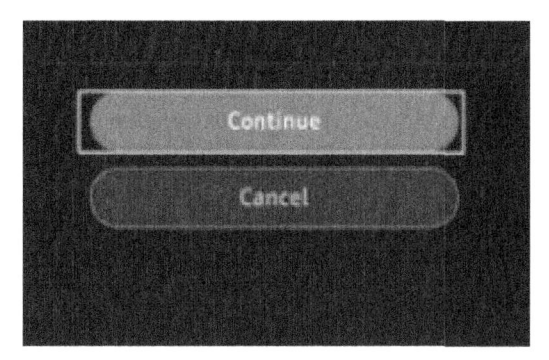

- Hit on "**Continue**."
- Then, choose "**Agree**."
- Hit on "**OK**."
- Next up, choose "**Allow**."

- Follow the prompts to proceed until the Galaxy Wearable main screen displays on your phone, indicating that your smartwatch is now set up.

Turn on Watch

- Long-tap the Home button on the side of the smartwatch till the Samsung logo shows up on the display. Then, wait for the Galaxy Watch to load.
- To power it off, long-tap the power button at the upper side of the smartwatch, then press "**Power off**."

Charge the Galaxy Watch

Having your Galaxy Watch fully charged is essential for getting the most out of it. It's advisable to plug it in for a charge the moment you unwrap it or after it hasn't been used for several days.

Once your battery runs low, the battery indicator at the top will become empty.

- Plug one part of the smartwatch's charger into an adaptor, then have the

- other end plugged into the charger's port.
- Follow up by placing the Galaxy Watch on the dock. While doing this, makes rue that the back is placed in the middle of the wireless charging dock
- When the Galaxy Watch starts charging, a red light will appear on the dock's LED display.

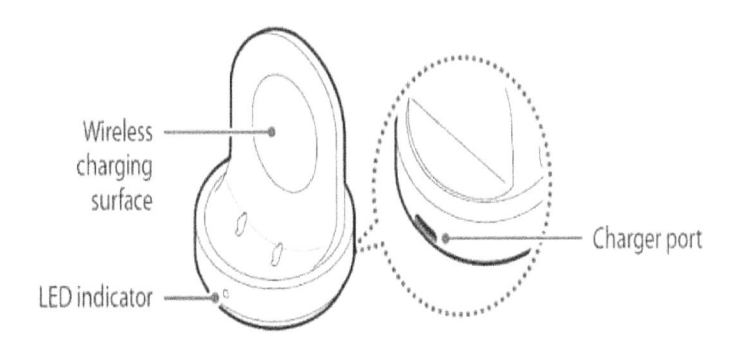

[Diagram: Wireless charging surface, LED indicator, Charger port]

- When completely charged, it'll flash a green light.

Charge with Wireless PowerShare

Your Samsung Galaxy smartphone can also serve as a charger for your smartwatch.

- Drag down from the upper area of your smartwatch screen to view the Quick settings.
- Press the Wireless PowerShare icon to activate it.
- Go ahead and position the smartwatch at the middle of the back of your Samsung Galaxy smartphone.

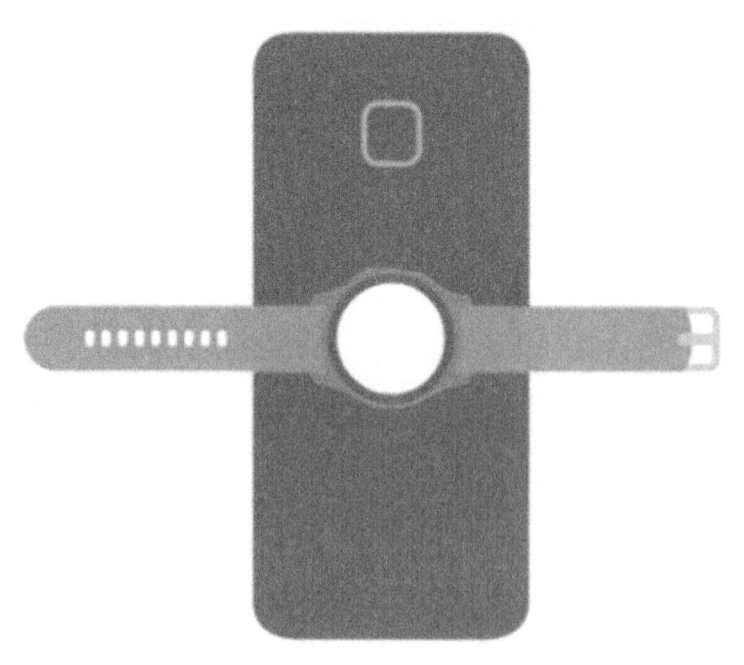

- Once a blue LED flashes, it indicates that the Wireless PowerShare is active. Hold on for the smartphone to vibrate. You should then see a red LED.
- After the smartwatch is charged, disconnect from the smartphone, then disable Wireless PowerShare.

Back up Galaxy Watch

By backing up your smartwatch, you'll be saving a copy of it on the cloud so that you can easily retrieve it when needed, even when you don't have your Galaxy Watch anymore.

- Press the home button of your smartwatch to load the app list.
- Hit on the Settings app.
- Move down, then press "**Account and backup**."

- Thereafter, choose "**Back up data**."

- From there, press "**Show on phone**."

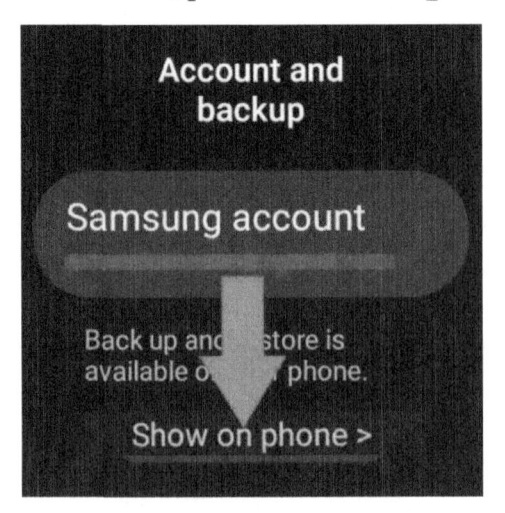

- The Galaxy Wearable app will load on your smartphone, right on the "**Account and Backup**" page. If that doesn't happen automatically, head to the Galaxy Wearable application on your connected smartphone.

- After that, choose "**Watch settings**."
- Move down and press "**Account and backup**."

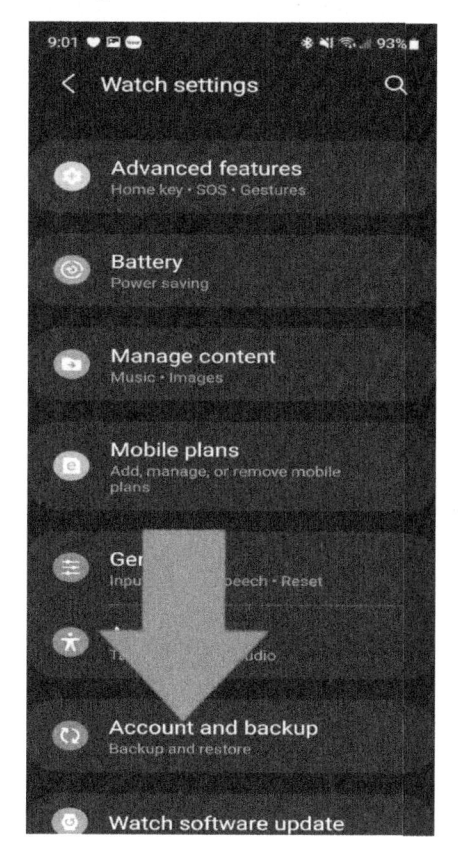

- Then, hit "**Back up data**."

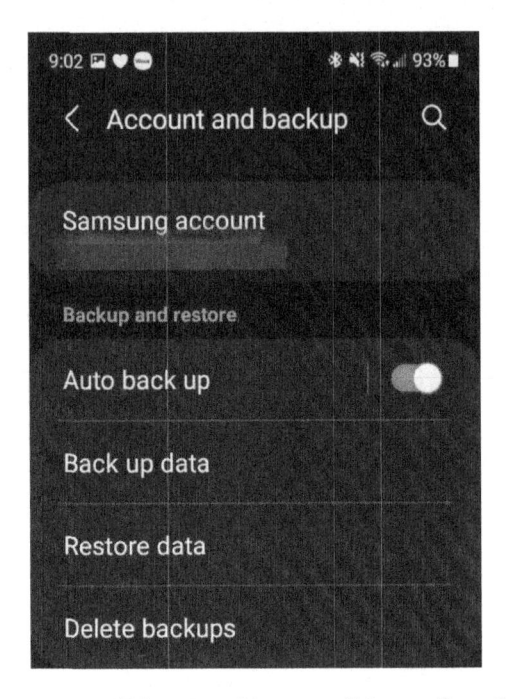

- Proceed by toggling on "**Auto back up**" to activate automatic backup.
- Go ahead and choose the data you desire to back up, then press **Start**.

Reset your Galaxy Watch

Performing a factory reset will make your smartwatch revert to its original factory settings and applications. Ensure you've made a backup of your data before proceeding.

- Press the home button of your smartwatch to load the app list.

- Hit on the Settings app.
- Move down, then press "**Account and backup**."
- Now, hit on "**Reset**."

Back up data

If you reset, all personal information will be erased from your watch.

Reset

- Here, press "**Reset**."

> **Reset**
>
> Back up your data to Samsung Cloud before resetting. You can restore it later on this watch or a new watch.

- Wait while your Galaxy Watch removes your data and changes everything to factory settings.

Enable Mobile Networks

If you own the LTE version of the Galaxy smartwatch, you can adjust its mobile network configuration.

- Press the home button on the side of the smartwatch to see the application menu.
- Press the Settings app.
- Thereafter, press "**Connections**."
- Next up, hit "**Mobile networks**."

- Follow up by choosing an option from the next screen.
- Move down, then press "**Mobile plans**" to preview the available mobile plans for your Galaxy Watch.

Chapter Two

Change Brightness

If your watch's screen is too bright or dark, you can adjust it to your liking.

- Press the home button on the side of the smartwatch to see the application menu.
- Choose the Settings app.
- Thereafter, press "**Display**."
- Here, press "**Brightness**."
- Press the + or − button to increase/decrease the screen brightness.

Change Screen Timeout

With screen timeout, you can adjust the duration it will take before your watch's screen sleeps.

- Press the home button on the side of the smartwatch to see the application menu.
- Choose the Settings app.
- Thereafter, press "**Display**."
- Now, select "**Screen timeout**."
- Next up, choose the timeframe before your watch's screen will go to sleep after inactivity.

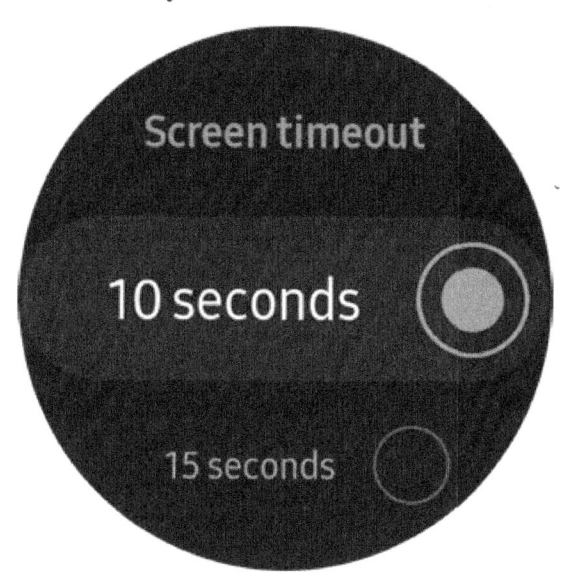

Enable Always on Display

To keep your smartwatch's display from going to sleep, simply activate "Always on Display."

- Press the home button on the side of the smartwatch to see the application menu.
- Choose the Settings app.
- Thereafter, press "**Display**."
- Then, press and toggle on "**Always on Display**."

Clear Storage

Once you notice some unnecessary items on your smartwatch are taking up too much storage, you can get rid of them.

- Move to your smartphone and launch the Galaxy Wearable application.
- In there, press "**Watch settings**."
- Then, select "**About watch**."
- Here, press "**Storage**."
- Hit on "**Images**."
- Choose the photographs you desire to remove.
- Thereafter, press "**Delete**."
- Press "**Delete**" again.
- After which, press "**Audio**," then choose the desired audio files to delete. Press "**Delete**."

Change the Wrist Orientation

The wrist orientation indicates on which hand you'll be wearing your Galaxy smartwatch. If you decide to alternate between the right and left hands, ensure you change the settings on the watch as well to reflect which hand you're wearing it on.

- Press the home button on the side of the smartwatch to see the application menu.
- Choose the Settings app.
- In there, press "**Display**."
- Thereafter, press "**General**."
- After which, select "**Orientation**."
- Hit on "**Right**" or "**Left**" underneath the "**Wrist**" heading.
- Press "**Right**" or "**Left**" underneath the button position. Ensure to put the smartwatch on the chosen hand to get accurate readings during measurement.

Enable Bluetooth

- Press the home button on the side of the smartwatch to see the application menu.
- Press the Settings app.
- Thereafter, press "**Connections**."
- Then, press "**Bluetooth**."
- Followed by turning on the Bluetooth toggle.
- After your smartwatch's Bluetooth is enabled, it'll become visible to nearby Bluetooth devices.

Enable Disconnection Alerts

Disconnection alerts inform you whenever your watch gets unpaired from Bluetooth.

- Press the home button on the side of the smartwatch to see the application menu.
- Press the Settings app.
- Thereafter, press "**Connections**."
- Here, choose "**Disconnection alerts**."
- Followed by pressing an alert style to select it.

Enable Wi-Fi

Need to pair your Galaxy Watch to a Wi-Fi network? Then, do this:

- Press the home button on the side of the smartwatch to see the application menu.
- Press the Settings app.
- Thereafter, press "**Connections**."
- Now, press "**Wi-Fi**." Press the toggle to turn it on.
- Thereafter, press "**Wi-Fi Networks**."
- Press the network you desire to pair with.
- Press "**Password**" to fill in the network's password if it's encrypted.
- Now, press "**Enter Password**."
- Afterward, press "**Done**."

Pair Bluetooth Headphones with Watch

To listen to music via headset, you can pair your smartwatch with a Bluetooth headset.

- Press the home button on the side of the smartwatch to see the application menu.
- Choose the Settings app.
- Thereafter, press "**Connections**."
- Now, press "**Bluetooth**."

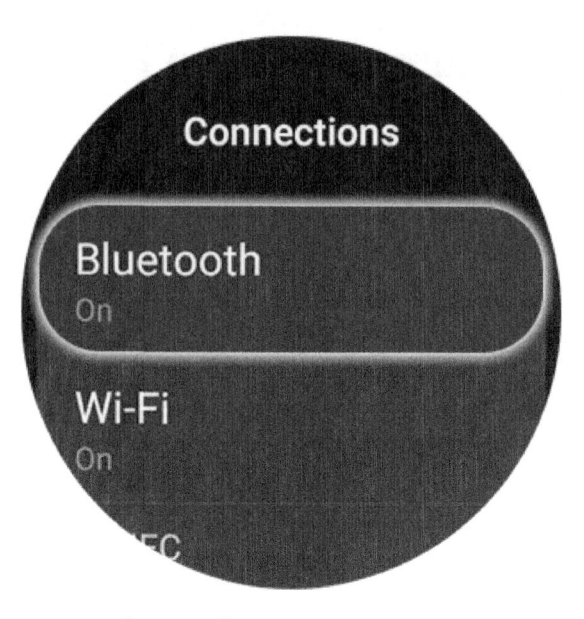

- Toggle on Bluetooth.
- Follow up by turning on the pair mode for the headphone.
- Then, press "**Bluetooth audio**" or "**Bluetooth headset**."
- Move on by selecting your desired Bluetooth headphone.
- Once the pairing is complete, press the Settings icon beside the paired Bluetooth headphones to activate "**Call audio**" and "**Media audio**."
- Hit on "**Unpair**" to disconnect your headphone from the watch.

Enable Airplane Mode

Whenever you activate airplane mode on your smartwatch, you'll be unable to use wireless services like Bluetooth, phone calls, etc.

- Press the home button on the side of the smartwatch to see the application menu.
- Choose the Settings app.
- Thereafter, press "**Connections**."

- Swipe up, then press the toggle beside the "**Airplane mode**" option to enable/disable it.

Enable Power Saving Mode

When you set your smartwatch to power-saving mode, some wireless services will be disabled, but you'll still receive calls and alerts. This mode helps your battery last longer.

- Press the home button on the side of the smartwatch to see the application menu.
- Choose the Settings app.

- Thereafter, press "**Battery**."
- Next up, press "**Power saving**."
- Press the checkmark.
- If you need to disable it, look to the bottom, then press "**Turn off**" and hit the checkmark icon.

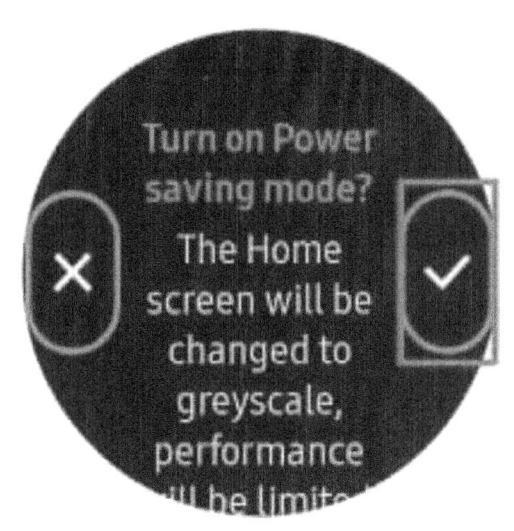

Add Screen Lock

By adding a PIN or lock pattern to encrypt your Galaxy smartwatch, only you or someone who has your PIN or lock pattern can unlock the device.

- Press the home button on the side of the smartwatch to see the application menu.
- Press the Settings app.
- Thereafter, press "**Security and privacy**."
- Next up, press "**Lock**."
- Here, press "**Type**."
- Follow up by selecting PIN or Pattern to encrypt your smartwatch.
- If you don't need a lock screen, press "**None**."

Chapter Three

Adjust the Watch's Face

The watch face of your smartwatch can be changed to reflect your taste.

Option 1:

- Put on the smartwatch on your wrist.
- Long-tap the current watch face to make it zoom out.

- The tile menu will load, showing the many watch faces that can be used with your watch. Choose your desired watch face by swiping left or right.

Option 2:

- Head to the Galaxy Wearable application on your smartphone.
- In there, press the "**Watch faces**" button.

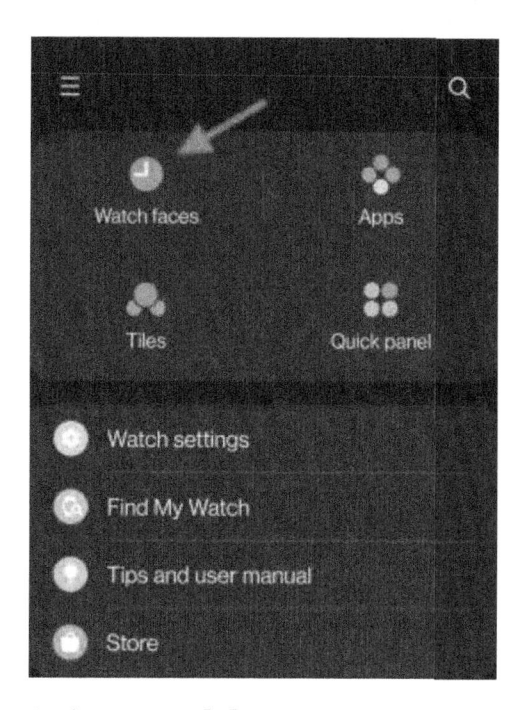

- Swipe up and down to press on your desired watch face.

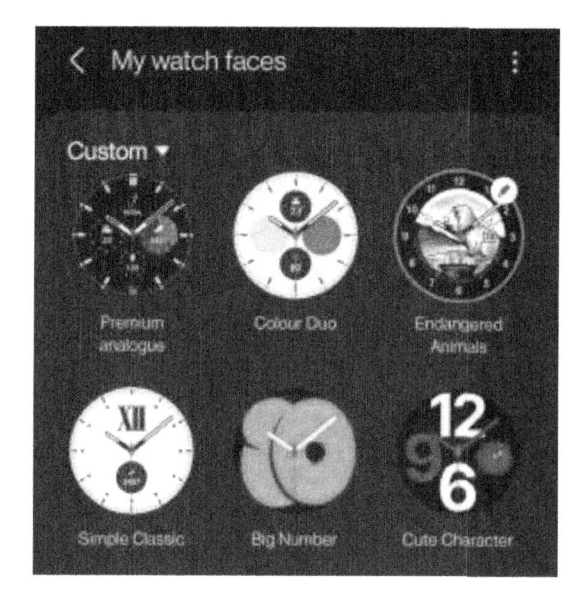

31

Personalize the Watch Face

Some watch faces come with complications," which enable you to add certain features like heart rate, blood pressure, step count, etc.

Option 1:

- Put on the smartwatch on your wrist.
- Long-tap the current watch face to make it zoom out.
- Thereafter, press "**Customize**."

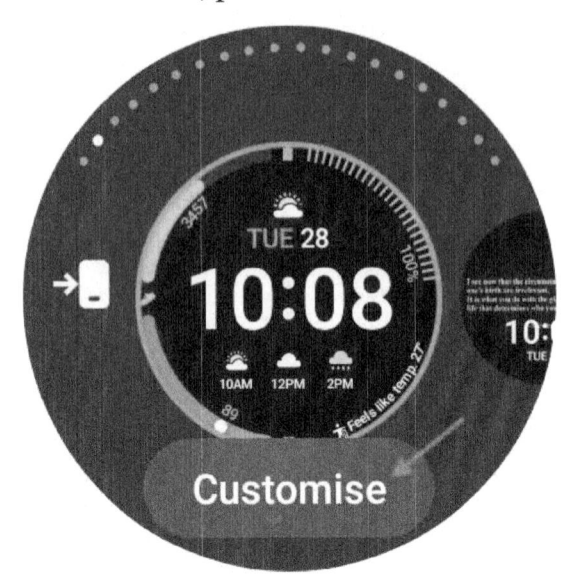

- A display will pop up where you can apply changes to the watch face and add complications. An options menu appears when you press a complication you wish to edit.

- Choose your desired complication.

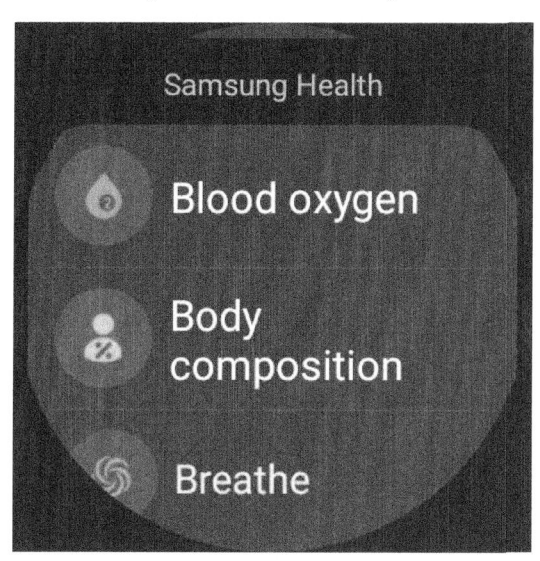

- Swipe up, then press "**OK**."

- The watch face will now display the new complication.

Option 2:

- Head to the Galaxy Wearable application on your smartphone.
- In there, press the "**Watch faces**" button.
- Beneath the watch's face name, press "**Customize**."

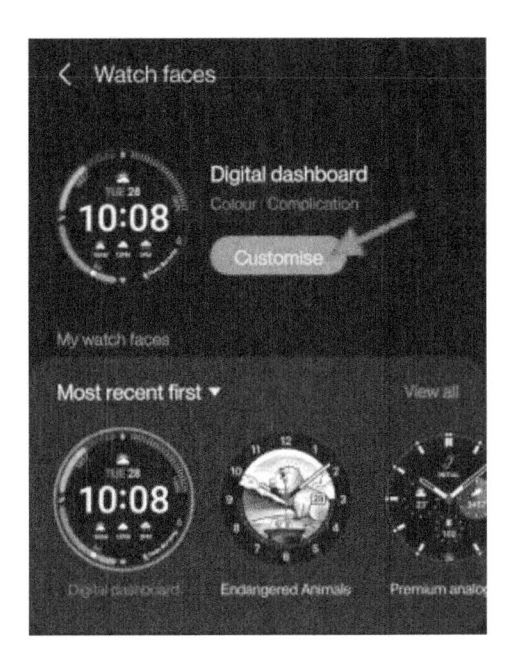

- Proceed by choosing from the displayed complications.

- Hit on the option you desire to change.

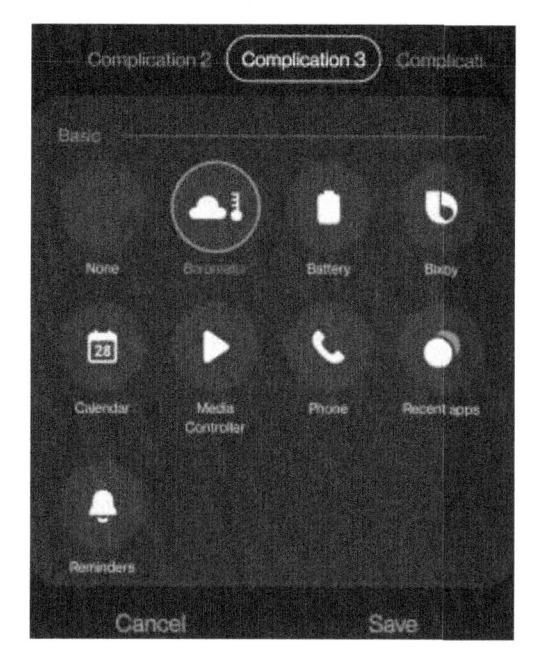

- Then, press "**Save**."

Add your Photo as Watch Face

Rather than using the default watch faces, you can also use your personal images as watch faces.

- Head to the Galaxy Wearable application on your smartphone.
- In there, press the "**Watch faces**" button.
- Head to the "**Basic**" section.

- Right there, press "**My Photo+**."

- Then, press "**Customize**."

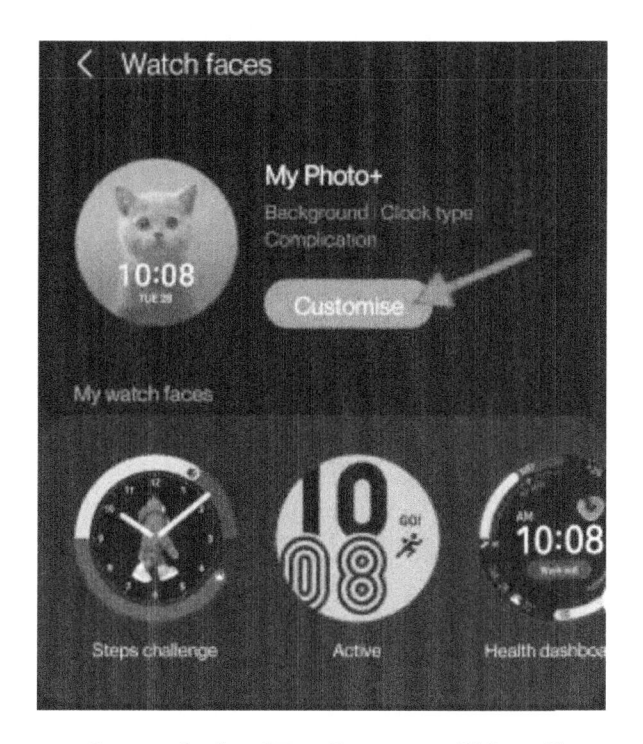

- Beneath the "**Background**" heading, press "**Camera**" or "**Gallery**."

- Press the photo you desire to use.
- Afterward, press "**Done**."
- Proceed by editing the photo watch face to your liking.
- Thereafter, choose "**Done**."
- Move ahead and customize the clock, as well as add complications.
- Then, select "**Save**."

- The chosen watch face will now display on your smartwatch.

Chapter Four

Setting up Bixby

Samsung created Bixby, a voice assistant. It's used to issue voice commands, answer questions, and fetch data online.

- Press the home button on the side of the smartwatch to see the application menu.
- Hit on the Bixby app.
- Go ahead and authorize the required Bixby permission.
- Go through the prompts to finish it.
- After the setup is over, you can then summon Bixby and ask it whatever you want. For instance, "Bixby, play Drake's song."

Enable Voice Commands

Ensure you turn on voice wake-up so that Bixby will work the way it should.

- Press the home button on the side of the smartwatch to see the application menu.
- Hit on the Bixby app.
- Press the compass button.
- Then, choose "**Settings**."

- Thereafter, press "**Voice wake-up**." Press the switch to activate it.
- Press the switch beside the "**Speak**" option to speak your command after saying the "Bixby" phrase.
- Go back to the last screen, then press "**Voice response**." Hit on "**Always**" Or "**Hands-free only**."

Setting up Google Assistant

Google Assistant is owned by Google, and just like Bixby, it is a voice assistant. You make it the default voice assistant if desired.

- Press the home button on the side of the smartwatch to see the application menu.
- Hit on the Play Store app.

- Move ahead by typing in the search box to find Google Assistant.

- Click on Assistant, then press "**Update**."

43

Enable Google Assistant

You can replace Bixby by using Google Assistant as your watch's default voice assistant.

- Press the home button on the side of the smartwatch to see the application menu.
- Hit on the Assistant app.
- In there, press "**Get started**."
- Thereafter, press "**Open on phone to activate**."
- From your smartphone, press "**Activate**."

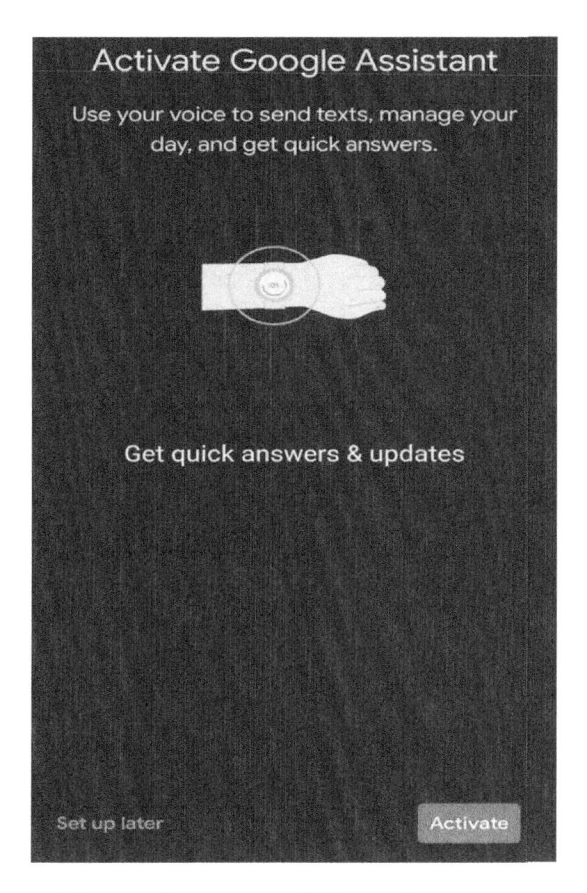

- Thereafter, press "**Next**."

- Then, press "**I agree**."
- If you prefer to have Google save your recorded audio anytime you give a command, press "**Start saving audio**." To decline, press "**Not now**."
- Then, press "**Turn on**."
- Once the setup is over, to trigger Google Assistant and ask questions, simply say "Hey Google," then say your command.

Adjust the Home Key Settings

You can change the watch's settings so that pressing and holding the Home button brings up Google Assistant instead of Bixby.

- Press the home button on the side of the smartwatch to see the application menu.
- Hit on the Settings app.
- Thereafter, press "**Advanced features**."

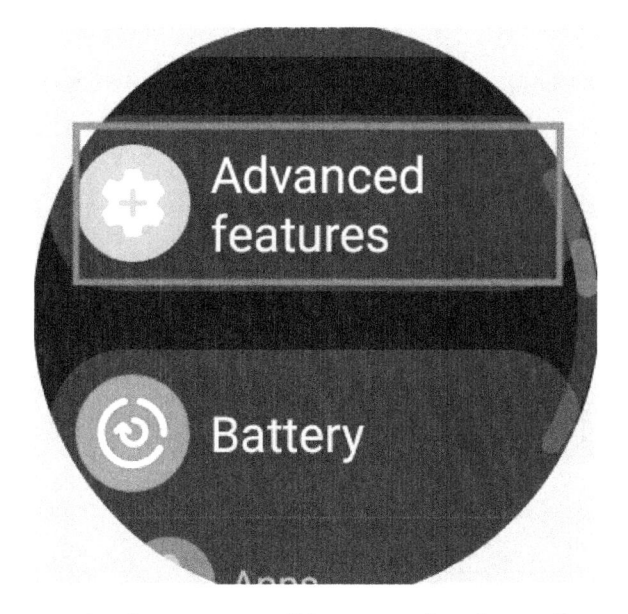

- In there, press "**Customize keys**."

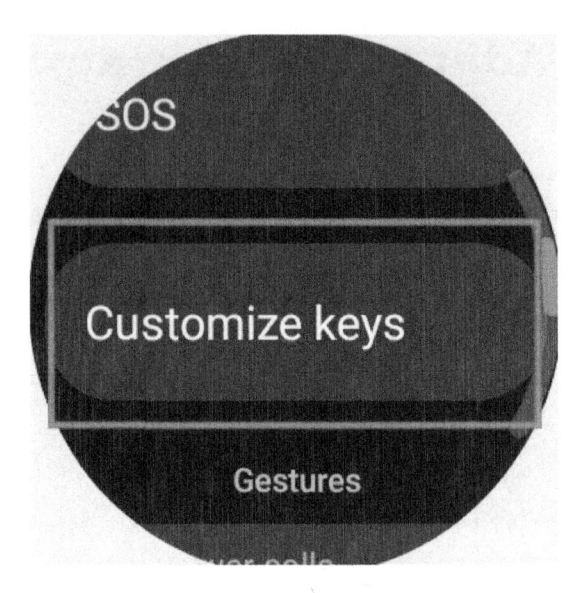

- After which, tap the "**Press and hold**" option underneath the "**Home key**" submenu.

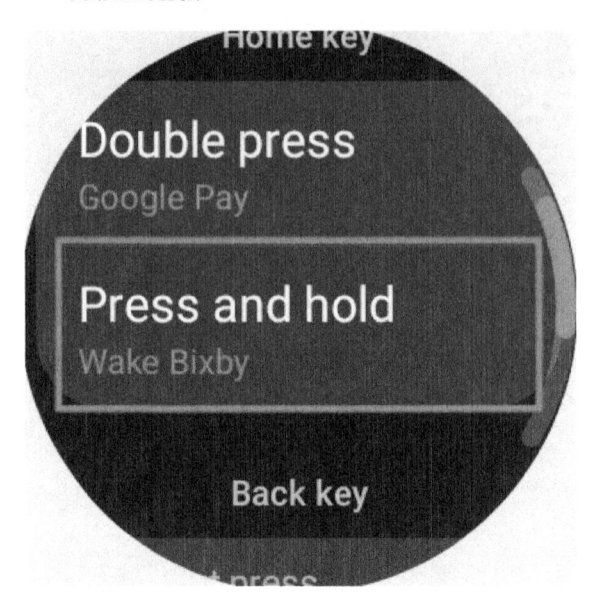

- Right there, press "**Assistant**."

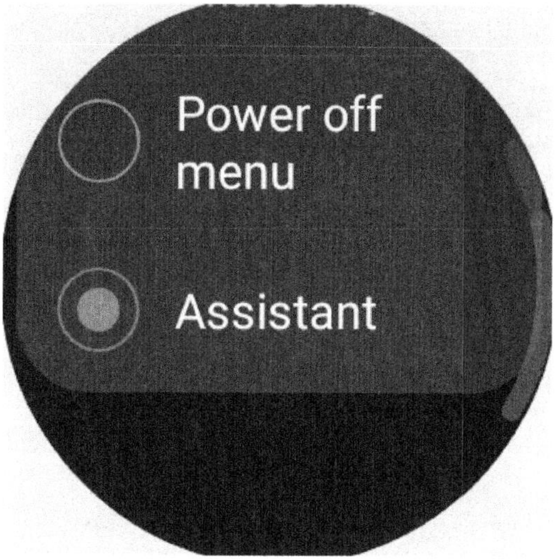
Power off menu
Assistant

Chapter Five

Change when to Show Alerts

The Galaxy smartwatch lets you schedule alerts to appear at times that are most convenient for you.

- Head to the Galaxy Wearable application on your smartphone.
- In there, press the "**Watch faces**."

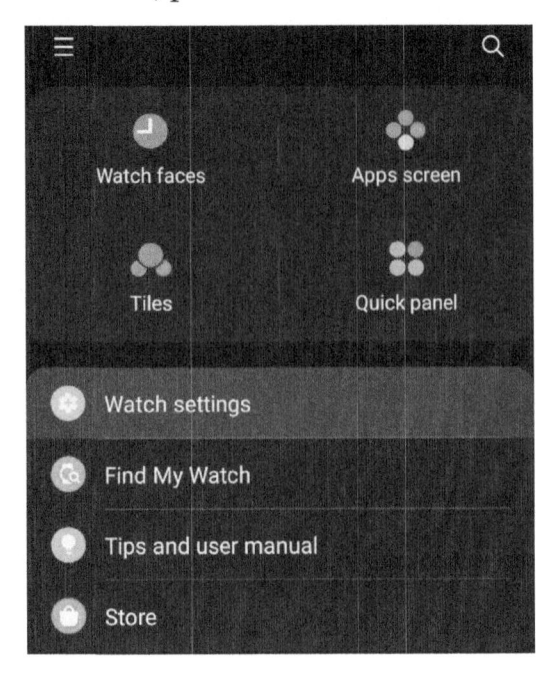

- Thereafter, select **Notifications**.

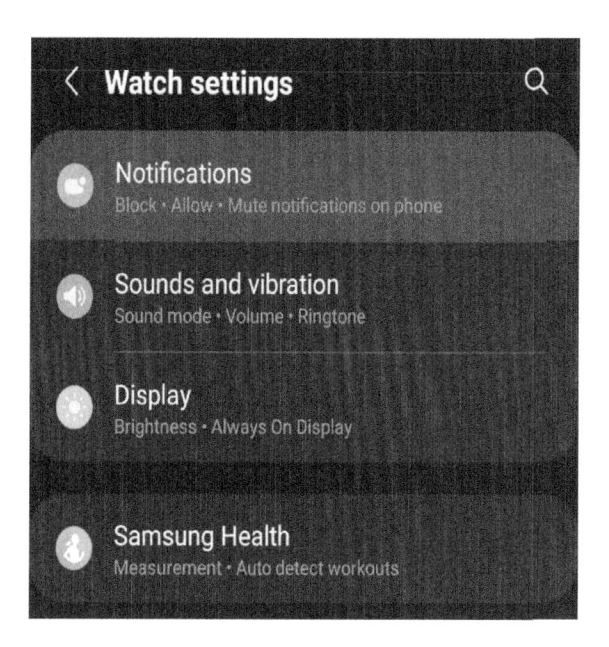

- Go ahead and press "**Show phone notifications on watch**."

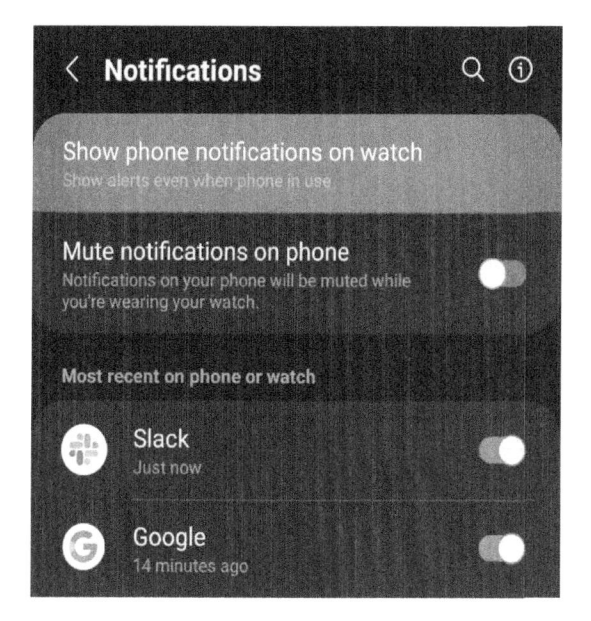

- Thereafter, choose from the displayed options.

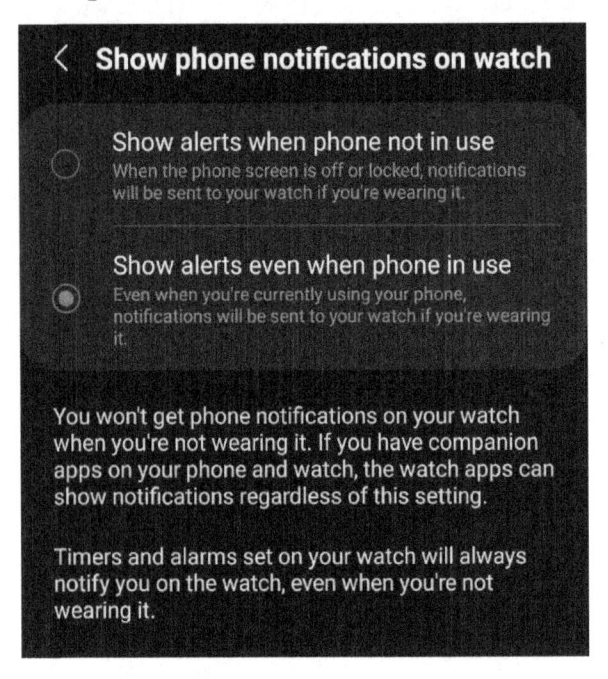

Select Apps that can Send Alerts

You have control over the application you wish to receive alerts from; you can disable the rest if needed.

- Move to the Galaxy Wearable application on your smartphone.
- In there, press the "**Watch faces**."

- Thereafter, press "**Notifications**."
- Move to the section that displays individual apps, then choose "**More**."
- Go ahead and find the application that you desire to disable from sending an alert to your smartphone.
- press the application switch to enable or disable it.
- To apply these settings to new applications, press "**Advanced Notifications**" from the "Notifications" menu. Proceed by pressing the switch beside the "**Turn on for new apps**" button to enable or disable it.

Enable Water Lock

When you toggle on Water Lock Mode, it'll eject water that gets into your Galaxy Watch whenever you go swimming. It prevents water from getting into the smartwatch.

Option 1:

- Move to the Galaxy Wearable application on your smartphone.
- In there, press the "**Watch faces**."
- Thereafter, press "**Advanced features**."

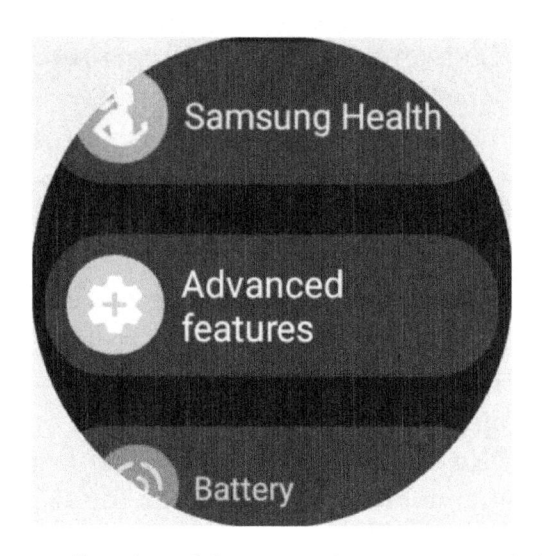

- Following this, press "**Water Lock**."

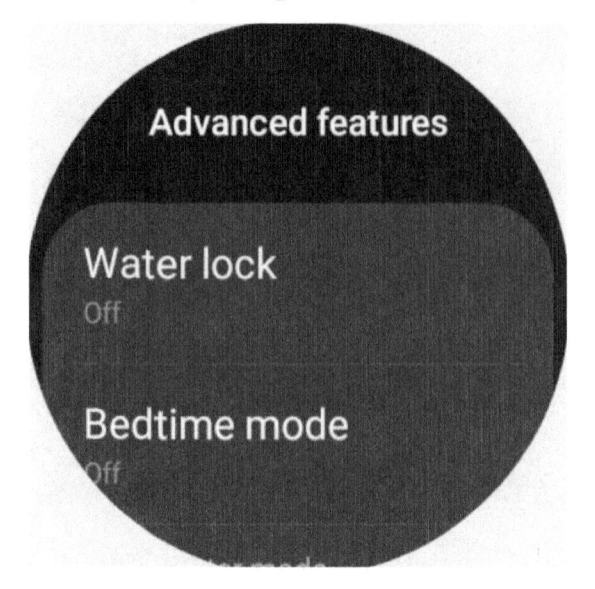

- After which, press the "**Water Lock**" toggle.

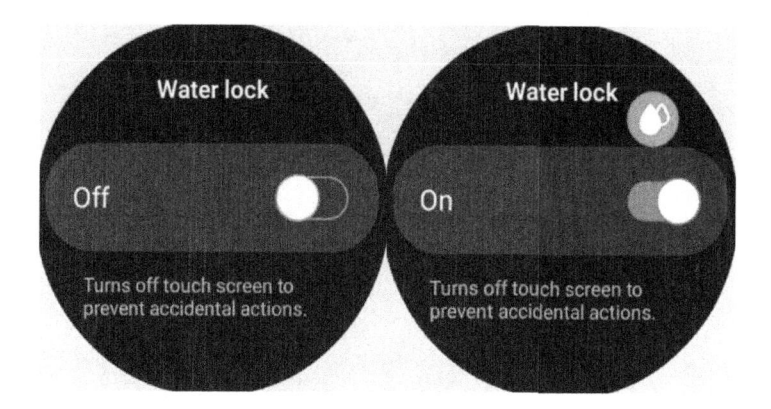

- After swimming, long-tap the home button for three seconds to deactivate the water lock.

- After that, press the home button again to stop.

Option 2:

- Swipe downward from the upper area of the swatch's main screen.

- Then, press the Water lock icon.

Enable Bedtime Mode

Bedtime mode disables all notifications so that you can sleep without being interrupted. However, the alarm can still ring.

- Move to the Galaxy Wearable application on your smartphone.
- In there, press the "**Watch faces**."
- After which, press "**Advanced features**."
- Thereafter, press "**Bedtime mode**."

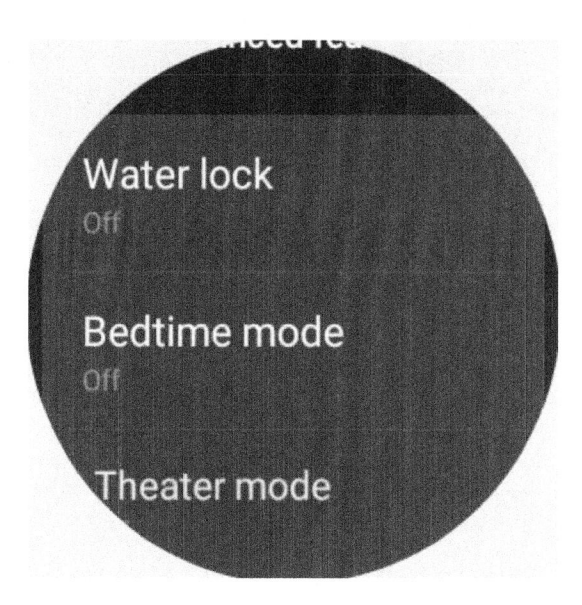

- Press the toggle beside "**Bedtime mode**" to activate it.

- If needed, press the toggle beside "**Turn it on as a schedule.**"

- Thereafter, press "**Days**" to choose your desired days.
- Press "**Set Schedule**" to pick a time.

Enable Theater Mode

Theater mode mutes every alert, helping you stay focused.

- Move to the Galaxy Wearable application on your smartphone.
- In there, press the "**Watch faces**."
- Then, press "**Advanced features**."
- Thereafter, press "**Theater mode**."
- After which, press "**Turn on Now**."

- Go ahead and choose your desired time.

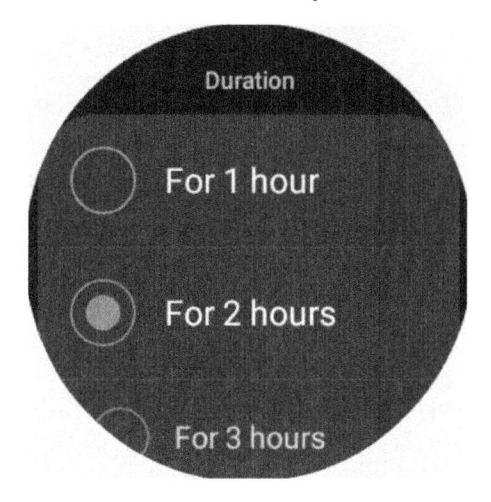

Enable Do Not Disturb

- Head to the Galaxy Wearable application.

- Then, press "**Watch faces**."
- Thereafter, press "**Advanced features**."
- Right there, press "**Theater mode**."
- After which, choose "**Do Not Disturb**."
- Next up, press "**Turn on now**."
- Hit on "**Turn on as scheduled**" to Y schedule DND.
- Then, choose and customize "**End Time**," "**Days**" and "**Start**."
- Thereafter, press "**Done**."

Change the Voice Assistant's Language

You can change the language you use when speaking to voice assistants like Google Assistant or Bixby.

- Press the home button on the side of the smartwatch to see the application menu.
- Choose Bixby or the S-Voice app.
- Then, press "**Settings**."
- In there, press "**Language and voice style**."
- Next up, press "**Voice style**" or "**Language**."

- Thereafter, choose an option.

Change the Voice Input Language

If you'd rather change the voice input language when using the keyboard's voice input, this will not affect the input language of the voice assistant.

- Press the home button on the side of the smartwatch to see the application menu.
- Choose the Settings app.
- Now, press "**General**."
- Thereafter, press "**Input**."

- In there, press "**Keyboard list and default**."
- Next up, press "**Samsung voice input**."
- After which, press "**Manage languages**."
- Move on by choosing or installing your desired language.

Change the Keyboard Input Language

The watch's keyboard supports several languages, and this can be adjusted as well. You can switch the keyboard to show French text if you speak French.

- Press the home button on the side of the smartwatch to see the application menu.
- Choose the Settings app.
- Now, press "**General**."
- Thereafter, press "**Samsung keyboard**."
- In there, press "**Manage languages**."
- Press the switch beside your desired language to make it the keypad's default language.

- Navigate to "**Available item**" or "**Available languages**." Right there, press the language to install it. Swipe horizontally to alternate between keyboard languages.

Set the Time and Date

- Press the home button on the side of the smartwatch to see the application menu.
- Choose the Settings app.
- Now, press "**General**."
- Thereafter, press "**Date and time**."
- Move on and press the toggle beside the "Automatic" option to automatically update the date and time. Or hit on "**Set**

time" and "**Set date**" to manually configure the date.

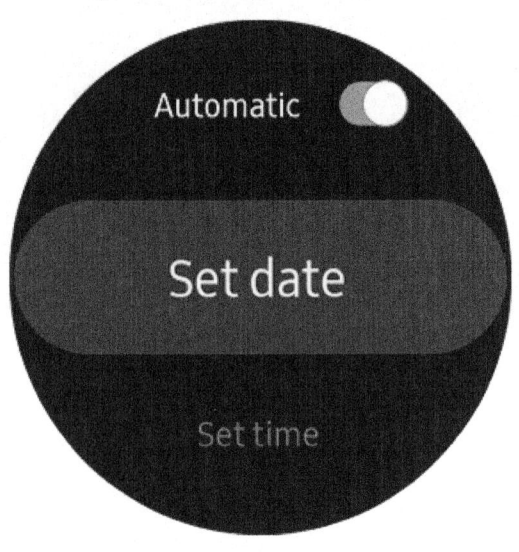

Chapter Six

Install Apps on your Watch

The Galaxy smartphone supports native application installation. But you must keep your smartphone close by and linked to the smartwatch at all times.

- Press the home button on the side of your smartwatch to see the app menu.
- Then, press the Google Play Store application.

- In there, choose "**My Apps**."

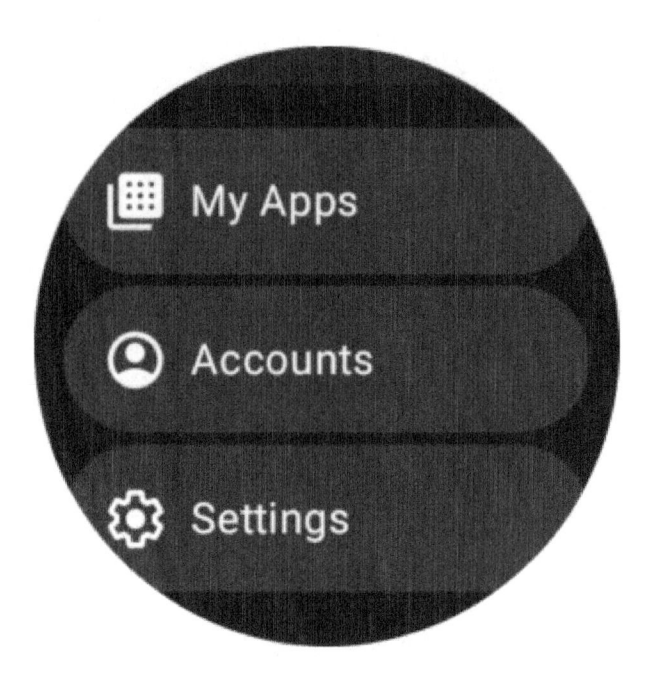

- Proceed by inserting the app's name on the search field to find it.
- When you locate the app, press "**Install**." If it's previously installed and needs to be updated, tap "**Update**."

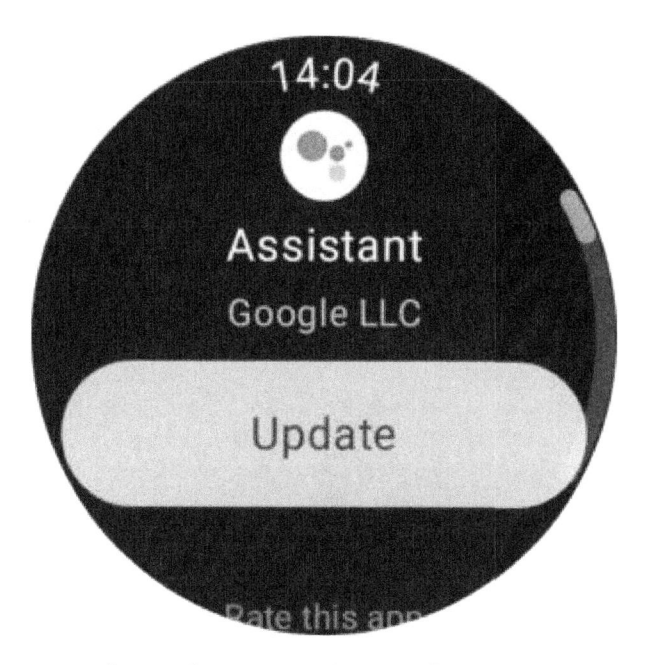

- Thereafter, press "**Open**" or "**Get started**."

Uninstall Apps

- Press the home button on the side of the smartwatch to see the app menu.
- Long-tap on the application you desire to uninstall.
- Thereafter, choose "**Uninstall**." If this option doesn't show up, then the application cannot be deleted.
- Then, press "**OK**."

Manage Apps Data

On the "Data Usage" menu, you'll be able to access the applications that are consuming a lot of data and restrict them.

- Press the home button on the side of the smartwatch to see the app menu.

- Press the Settings app.

- Thereafter, press "**Connections**."

- Then, press "**Data usage**."

- In there, tap "**Data limit**."
- Proceed by rotating the touch bezel to adjust the data limit.

- Press the tick button.

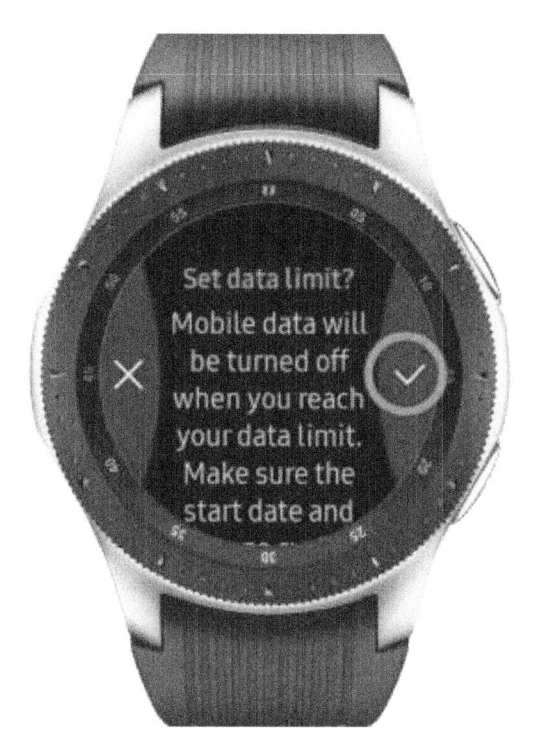

- Thereafter, press "**Data usage cycle**." Roll the touch bezel to adjust the cycle duration.

- Then, press "**Start date**" to adjust.
- Hit on "**Usage details**" and edit it.

Update your Watch Software

To ensure your smartwatch is running on the latest WearOS, it is advised that you check for updates and update it when available.

Option 1:

- Press the home button on the side of the smartwatch to see the application menu.

- Choose the Settings app.
- Then, press "**Software update**."

Option 2:

- Head to the Galaxy Wearable application on your smartphone.
- In there, press "**Watch settings**."
- Next up, press "**Watch software update**."
- Thereafter, press "**Download and install**."

Update Watch Apps

When you update your applications, you'll get the most recent bug fixes as well as the newest features.

- Press the home button on the side of the smartwatch to see the application menu.
- Now, choose the Play Store app.
- Thereafter, press "**My Apps**."
- Hit on the "**Update**" button (if available) beside the app to begin.
- Press the "**Update all**" button to install updates for all applications.

How to Use Google Maps

Google Maps is built-in on the Galaxy smartwatch; it can be used to get directions and navigate your terrain.

- Press the home button on the side of the smartwatch to see the application menu.
- Then, choose the Google Maps app.

- Right there, press the magnifying glass button to find a place.

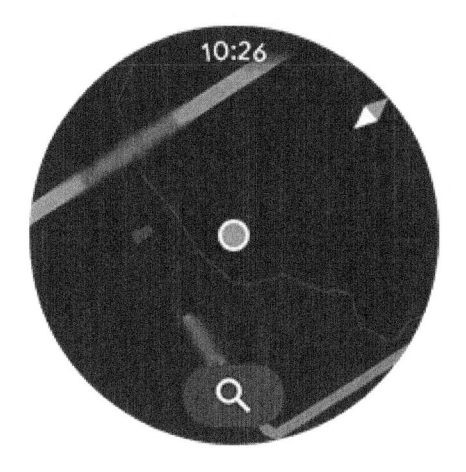

- Then, click the location you intend to visit from the listed ones or press the keyboard icon to search for a new location.

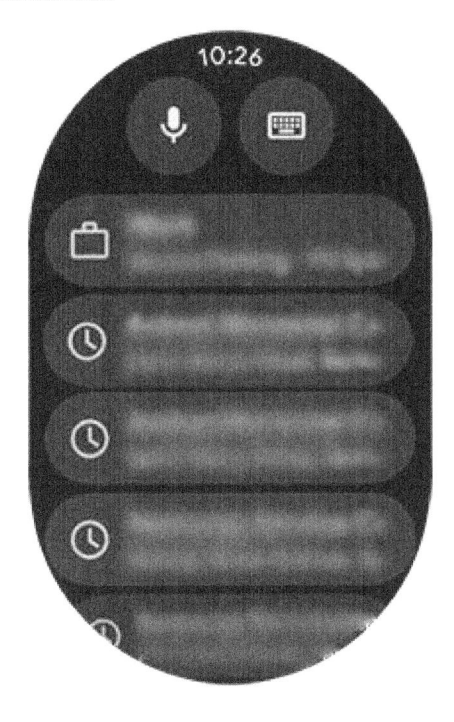

After which, select a travel method (walking, driving, etc.).

- Hold on for your smartwatch to fetch the quickest direction.

- Thereafter, follow the directions as stated on your smartwatch.

Using the Camera Controller

If you ever need to capture an image or scene with your Galaxy smartwatch, you can do so with the built-in Camera app.

- Press the home button on the side of the smartwatch to see the application menu.
- Hit on the Camera app.
- The smartwatch's display will mirror the screen of your smartphone.
- Press on your smartwatch to capture the image.

Using the Gallery App

The gallery app is where you'll find your captured photos.

- Press the home button on the side of the smartwatch to see the application menu.
- Then, choose the Gallery app.
- Swipe to see the image, and double-tap to zoom in and out.

- To delete it, long-tap on the image, then choose the "**Delete**" button.

Chapter Seven

Personalize Visibility Enhancements

On the visibility enhancement menu, you'll be able to make the content of your smartwatch more legible.

- Press the home button on the side of the smartwatch to see the application menu.
- Choose the Settings app.
- Thereafter, press "**General**."
- Right there, select "**Accessibility**."
- Now, press "**Visibility enhancements**."
- Right there, press on "**Font size**" and hit "**Medium**," "**Large**," or "**Small**."
- Hit on "**Add color filter**" to change the screen as well as the opacity of your watch.
- Press "**Color inversion**" to invert the screen's color. Or press other options to customize them.

Turn on TalkBack

TalkBack reads out whatever is displayed on your watch's screen.

- Press the home button on the side of the smartwatch to see the application menu.
- Choose the Settings app.
- Right there, press "**General**."
- Thereafter, select "**Accessibility**."
- In there, press "**TalkBack**." Press the switch to enable it.
- After doing so, your Galaxy Watch will provide audio descriptions of what's displayed on the screen.
- Once you press an option, you can hear some information about it. Press it twice to execute.
- If you need to customize "**Audio**" and "**Verbosity**," hit on "**Settings**."

Customize Hearing

On the "Hearing Enhancements" menu, you'll be able to adjust the audio and volume settings for your watch.

- Tap the home button on the side of your smartwatch to see the app menu.
- Then, press the Settings app.
- Thereafter, press "**General**."
- Right there, select "**Accessibility**."
- In there, press "**Hearing enhancements**."

- Go ahead and customize your desired settings from here.

Enable Accessibility Shortcut

A quicker way of getting to the Accessibility menu on your smartwatch is to enable triple-finger tapping.

- Tap the home button on the side of your smartwatch to see the app menu.
- Then, press the Settings app.
- Thereafter, press "**General**."
- Right there, select "**Accessibility**."
- Next up, press "**Advanced settings**."
- Thereafter, press the "**Two finger triple tap**" button underneath the "**Accessibility shortcuts**" heading.
- Proceed by pressing on your desired shortcut options.

Enable Double Press Key

On the "Double Press," you can configure your smartwatch so that it takes you to your frequently used applications whenever you double-tap the home button.

- Tap the home button on the side of your smartwatch to see the app menu.
- Then, press the Settings app.
- Thereafter, press "**General**."
- Right there, select "**Accessibility**."
- Next up, press "**Customize keys**."
- Thereafter, press "**Double press**."
- Go ahead and press the option you want the home button to launch when you double-tap it.

Chapter Eight

Set up Samsung Pay

With Samsung Pay, you wouldn't have to move about with your debit card anymore. You can conveniently make contactless payments at checkout directly on your wrist.

- Press the home button on the side of the smartwatch to see the application menu.
- Press the Samsung Pay app.
- Proceed by swiping horizontally across the display.
- Then, press the arrow to begin.

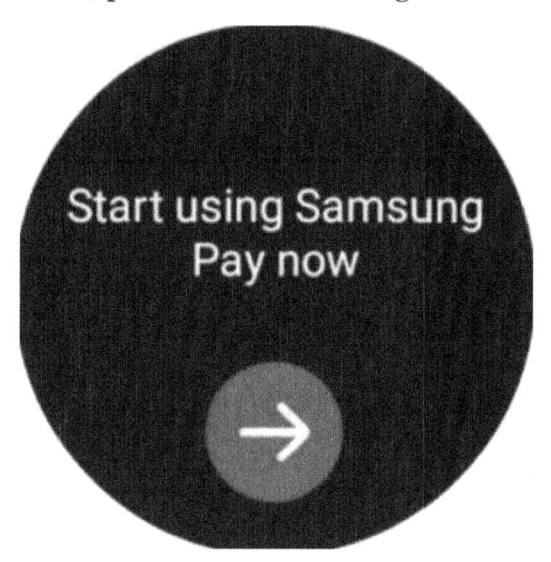

- Next up, press the + button on top of "**Add card**."

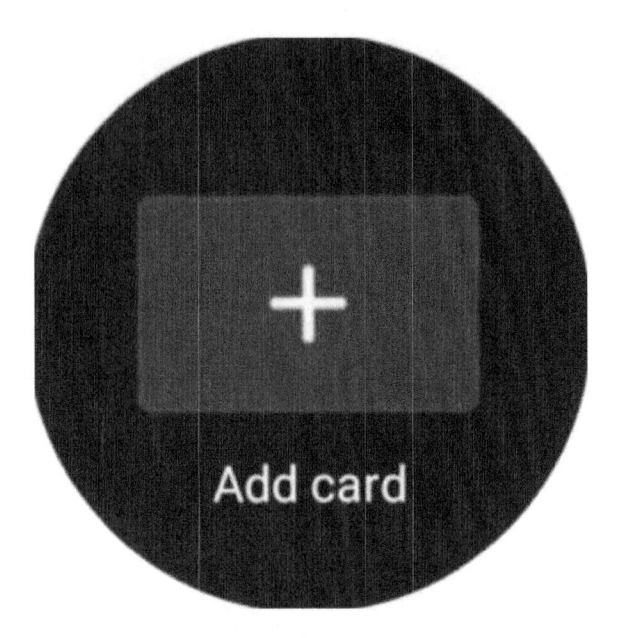

- Now, press "**OK**."

- Proceed by pressing "**Pattern**" or "**PIN**" which you'll use to authorize payment.

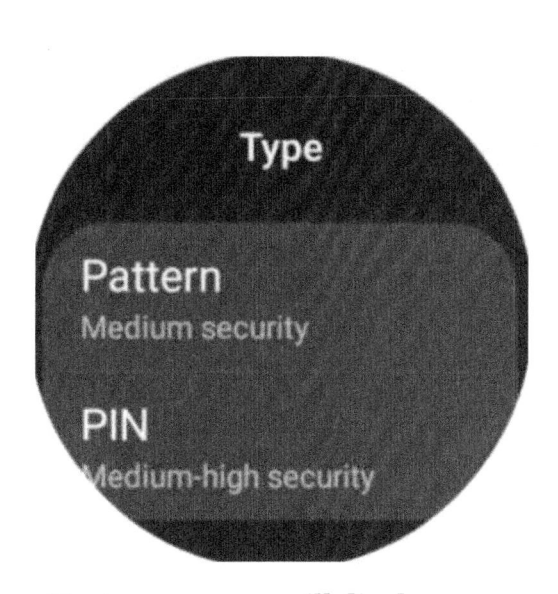

- Next up, a menu will display on your phone's screen.
- Thereafter, hit "**Add payment card**" or "**Import cards**" to pick the method you desire to use in adding your debit card.

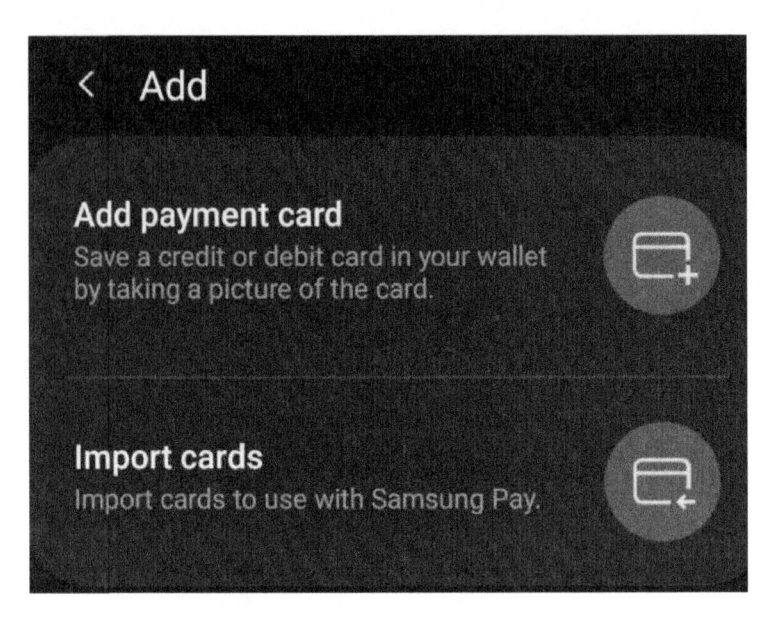

> **Add**
>
> **Add payment card**
> Save a credit or debit card in your wallet by taking a picture of the card.
>
> **Import cards**
> Import cards to use with Samsung Pay.

- Move on by placing your card within the camera's frame of your smartphone to automatically capture card details. Or, press "**Add card manually**" to insert the card details manually.
- Hit on "**Agree**."
- Go through the prompt and confirm the code sent to you through email or SMS.
- After setting up Samsung Pay on your smartwatch, you can start making purchases at any of the supported stores or online with your watch.
- When you need to check out, long-tap the back button on your Galaxy Watch to initiate your default card. Or swipe to choose another card.
- Thereafter, bring the watch's screen closer to the contactless payment terminal until payment is completed.

Enable NFC

NFC enables the sending of data between two devices that are in close proximity. To ensure Samsung Pay works appropriately, it is advised that you enable NFC.

- Press the home button on the side of the smartwatch to see the application menu.
- Press the Settings app.
- After which, press "**Connections**."
- Then, press "**NFC**." Press the switch to enable it.
- Hit on "**Payment**" to add the default payment application for your purchases.
- If you desire to use an open payment app, hit "**Pay**."
- In order to use NFC to make purchases, you'll need to enroll in the mobile payment service. Get in touch with your service provider to register.
- While paying, position the upper part of your watch's touchscreen on the credit card terminal.

You can choose which applications open up when you need to pay with NFC.

- Press the home button on the side of the smartwatch to see the application menu.
- Press the Settings app.

- After which, press "**Connections**."
- Then, press "**NFC**."
- Thereafter, press "**Others**."
- Proceed by selecting your desired app.

Add an Alarm

- Press the home button on the side of the smartwatch to see the application menu.
- Next up, press the Alarm app.
- Thereafter, hit on "**Add on watch**."
- Proceed by entering the time.
- Now, press "**Next**."
- Go ahead and choose the days you need the alarm to repeat.
- After which, press "**Save**."

Mute/Snooze an Alarm

- Hit on (×) to mute the alarm.
- Hit on (zZ) to snooze the alarm.

Remove an Alarm

- Press the home button on the side of the smartwatch to see the application menu.
- Next up, press the Alarm app.
- Press ⬤ to disable the alarm.
- To remove the alarm, long-tap on it, then press "**Delete**" from the context menu.

Use Stopwatch

- Press the home button on the side of the smartwatch to see the application menu.
- Right there, press the Stopwatch app.
- Next up, press "**Start**" to begin a countdown.
- Hit on "**Lap**" to track the lap times.
- To terminate the countdown, press "**Stop**."
- Hit on "**Resume**" to restart the countdown.
- Hit on "**Reset**" to reset the countdown to zero.

Add a Timer

- Press the home button on the side of the smartwatch to see the application menu.
- Hit the Timer app.
- Right there, choose time or press ⏳ to configure the timer.
- Press ▶ to begin.

Stop the Timer

- Hit on ✖ to cancel the timer.
- Press ↺ to restart.

Chapter Nine

Set up Workout

Your Galaxy smartwatch can help track your exercises and other health metrics such as sleep, heart rate, ECG, blood pressure, stress level, and so many others.

You can select from several types of exercises that you desire, and your watch can detect when you start the exercise.

- Press the home button of your Galaxy smartwatch to load the app list.
- Thereafter, choose the Samsung Health app.
- Right there, choose "**Exercise**."
- Next up, press "**Choose workout**."
- Proceed by allowing the required permissions.
- Choose your desired workout such as cycling, running, etc.
- Go through the onscreen prompt.
- Then, wait for the timer to elapse. After that, the workout will begin.
- Swipe horizontally on the display to pause, resume, or stop the exercise and select your preference.

Enable Continuous Heart Rate

If you prefer to have your heart rate tracked at all times, then you can choose the "Measure continuously" option from the "Heart rate" Menu.

- Press the home button of your Galaxy smartwatch to load the app list.
- Thereafter, choose the Samsung Health app.
- Move down, then press "**Settings**."
- Hit on "**Heart rate**" underneath the "**Measurement**" section.
- Thereafter, hit on "**Measure continuously**."

Measure Heart Rate Manually

Rather than continuous heart rate tracking, you can do it manually.

- Press the home button of your Galaxy smartwatch to load the app list.
- Thereafter, choose the Samsung Health app.
- Next up, choose "**Heart rate**."
- Then, press "**Measure**."

Get High or Low Heart Rate Alert

Your Galaxy Watch can drop notifications if your heart rate gets above or below a certain threshold.

- Press the home button of your Galaxy smartwatch to load the app list.
- Choose the Settings app.
- In there, press "**Samsung Health**."
- After which, press "**Heart rate**."
- Thereafter, press "**Low HR**" or "**High HR**" underneath the "**Hear rate alert**" section.

Enable Automatic Workout Detection

If you need your smartwatch to automatically detect when you start an exercise, then you should enable "Auto detect workouts."

- Press the home button of your Galaxy smartwatch to load the app list.
- Choose the Settings app.
- In there, press "**Samsung Health**."
- Thereafter, choose "**Auto detect workouts**."

- Hit on the switch beside any exercise to enable or disable auto-detect workouts.

Enable Snore Detection

Putting on your Galaxy smartwatch before bed is an easy way to keep tabs on how long and how well you sleep. The sleep tile will show you when you last snored, how long you slept last night, and provide you access to the sleep coaching features.

When you enable snore detection, your smartwatch can keep tabs on your snoring habit.

- Begin by swiping to the left on your Galaxy smartwatch until you see the **Sleep tile**. Tap on it.
- Check underneath the "**Snoring**" section, then choose "**Show on phone**."
- A menu will now open on your smartphone, press the toggle to activate "**Snore detection**."
- Thereafter, press "**Allow**."
- After which, press "**OK**."
- Check below the "**Detect snoring**" section, then press "**Once**" or "**Always**."

- Press the switch beside "**Record audio**" to track your snoring. Ensure your phone is by the bedside while you sleep.
- Check below the "**Delete audio recordings**" section, then press "**100**," "**7**," or "**31**" to indicate when the audio recording will be automatically deleted.
- To access your snore detection data, head to the Samsung Health application on your smartphone, then choose "**Sleep tracker**." Thereafter, press the data under "**Snoring**."

Enable Sleep Coaching

With sleep coaching, you can learn how to enhance your sleep.

- Head to the Samsung Health application.
- Then, press the "**Sleep**" tile.
- Press the triple vertical dots at the upper left.
- After that, press "**Sleep Coaching**."
- Go through the prompts to answer the displayed questions.
- Thereafter, you'll be assigned a "**Sleep Animal**" depending on your sleeping rhythm.
- Hit on "**Start**."

- Go through the prompts to finalize the setup.

Quit Sleep Coaching

- Head to the Samsung Health application.
- Then, press the "**Sleep**" tile.
- Press the triple vertical dots at the upper left.
- After that, press "**Sleep Coaching**."
- Thereafter, press "**More options**."
- Then, choose "**Quit coaching**."
- Hit on "**Quit coaching**" once more.

Enable Fall Detection

With fall detection turned on, your Galaxy smartwatch will deliver an emergency SOS notification to your emergency contacts when you've had a hard fall and are unable to get up after some time.

Option 1:

- Press the home button on your Galaxy smartwatch to load the app list.
- Thereafter, choose the Settings app.

- Then, press "**Advanced features**."
- After that, press "**SOS**."
- After which, press "**When hard fall detected**," then toggle it on.
- Go through the directions on your phone.

Option 2:

- Head to the Galaxy Wearable application on your smartphone.
- In there, choose "**Watch settings**."
- Then, hit on "**Advanced features**."
- After which, press "**SOS**."
- Thereafter, press "**When hard fall detected**."
- Press the switch at the top and confirm the required permissions.
- Choose the emergency contact that will be sent an SOS alert whenever a fall is detected.

Measure Stress

- Press the home button on your smartwatch to load the app list.
- Press the Samsung Health app.
- Swipe and press the "**Stress**."
- After that, choose "**Measure**."
- Proceed by authorizing the required permissions.

- Ensure the smartwatch is firmly clipped to your wrist. Be calm while the smartwatch tracks your stress level.
- After that, the result will be displayed. Press the **"Show on phone"** button.

Your smartwatch can be set to automatically monitor your stress levels at regular intervals.

- Press the home button on your smartwatch to load the app list.
- Press the Samsung Health app.
- Swipe and press the **"Stress."**
- Thereafter, press **"Measure continuously."**
- Also, you can begin breathing exercises after measuring your stress. Navigate to **"Breathe."** Press the + and - icons to change your desired cycles. After that, press **"Start."** Hit on **"Stop"** to stop.

Track your Steps

With your Galaxy smartwatch, you can monitor how many steps you walk daily.

- Press the home button on your smartwatch to load the app list.
- Press the Samsung Health app.
- Move down, then press **"Steps."**

- Move down, then choose "**Settings**."

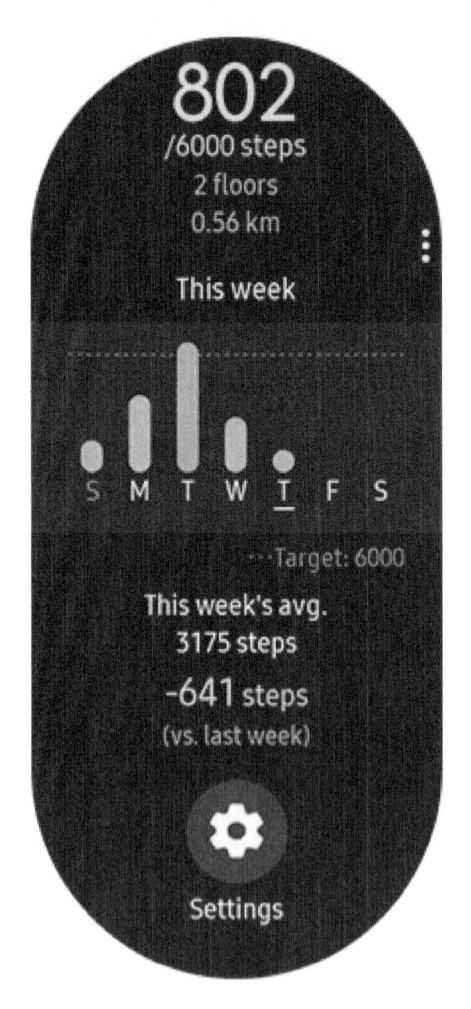

- Hit on "**Step Target**" to change the default daily step threshold.

Monitor Woman's Health

With the Samsung smartwatch, women can track their menstrual cycle and estimate when their next cycle will occur.

- Press the home button on your smartwatch to load the app list.
- Press the Samsung Health app.
- Move down, then press "**Women's Health**."

- Next up, press "**Enter period**." Then, fill in the date you started menstruating.

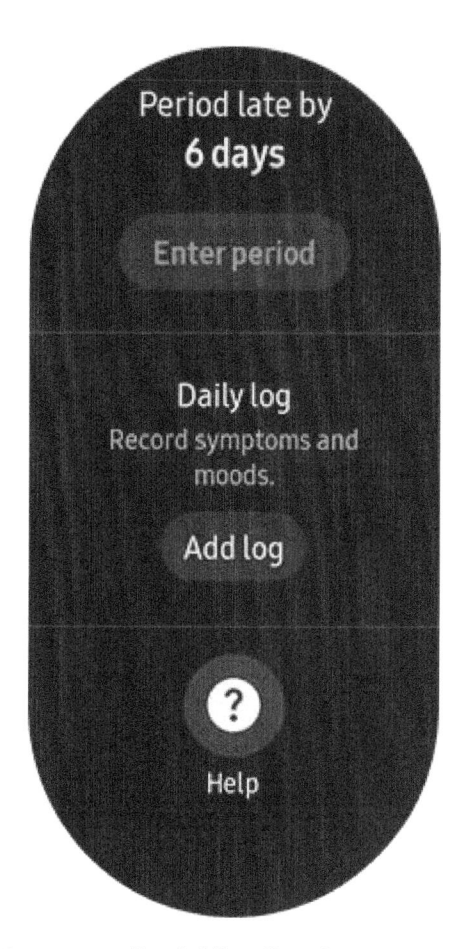

- Or, press "**Add log**" to insert a symptom.
- Choose the symptoms.

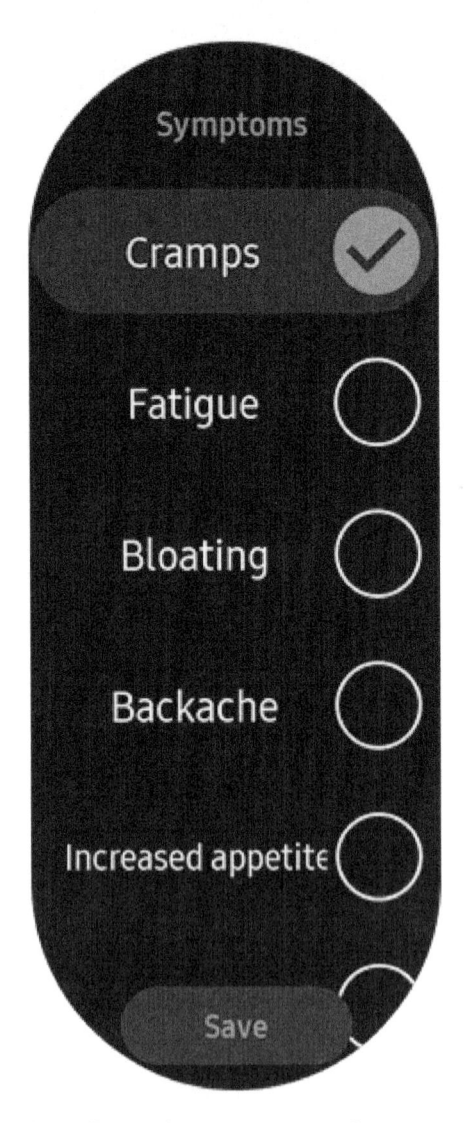

- After that, choose "**Save**."

Track your Body Composition

- Press the home button on your smartwatch to load the app list.
- Press the Samsung Health app.

- Next up, choose "**Body Composition**."

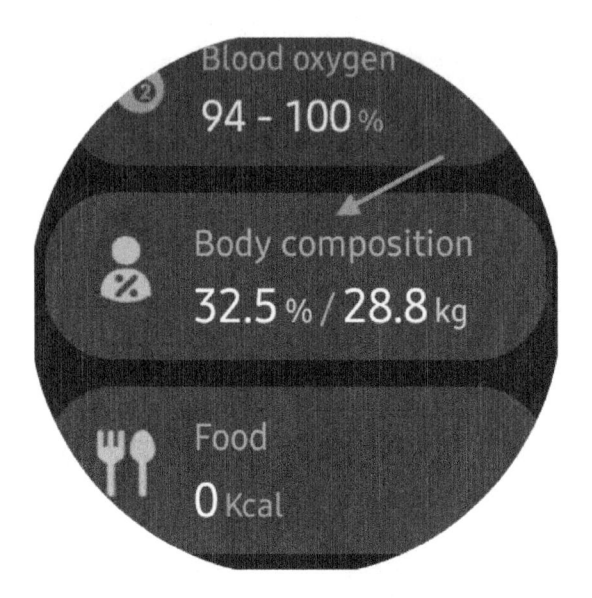

- Thereafter, press "**Measure**" to begin.

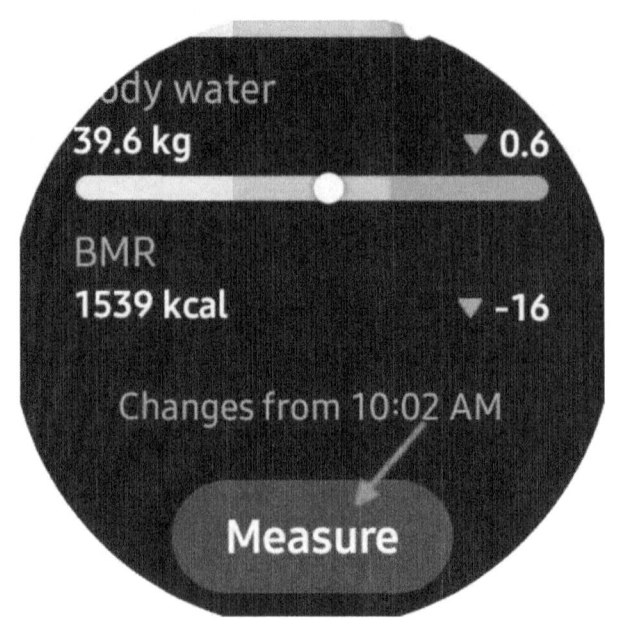

- Proceed by inserting your height, gender, and weight.

- Next up, press "**Confirm**."

- Go ahead and position your ring and middle fingers on the device's home and back buttons to commence. Be still for 15 seconds until the result comes up.

Disable Coaching Messages

- Press the home button on your smartwatch to load the app list.
- Press the Samsung Health app.
- Move down, then press "**Record your workout**."
- Thereafter, press the gear icon beside the "**Running Coach**" option.
- Toggle off "**Coaching Messages**."

Measure ECG

- Press the home button on your smartwatch to load the app list.
- Press the Samsung Health Monitor app.
- Next up, press "**Allow**."

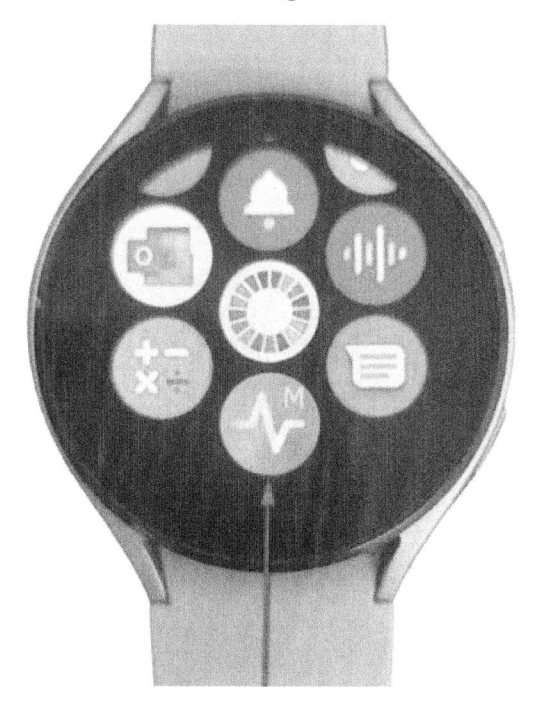

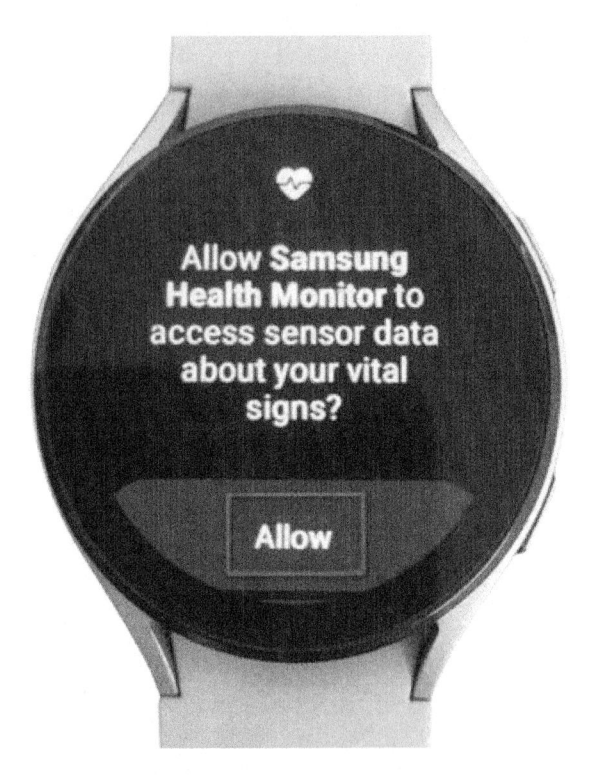

- Then, choose "**ECG**."

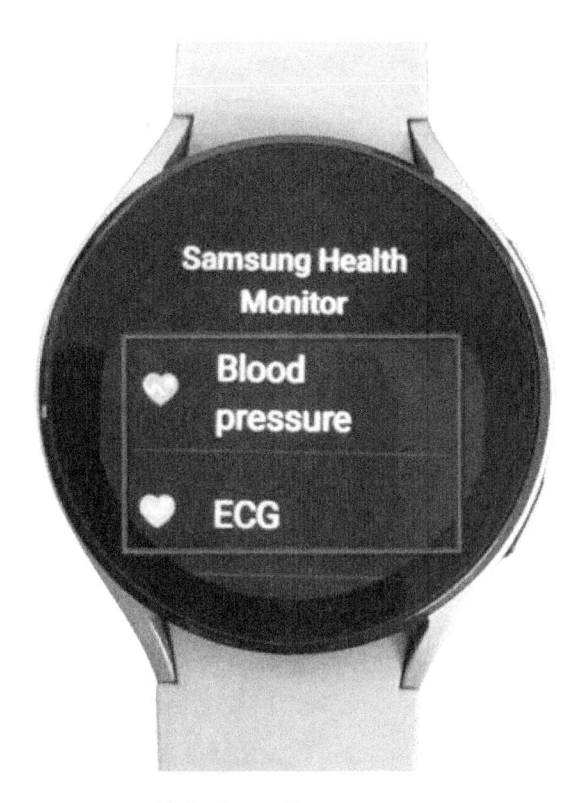

- Now, click "**OK**." Ensure your smartwatch is well-fitted to your wrist. After which, you should carefully place your finger at the top button of the watch.
- After now, your Galaxy Watch will track the ECG for 30 seconds and show if there are any symptoms of irregular heartbeat rhythm. If any, enter it to ensure that your watch knows more about your health.
- After the ECG tracking is over, head to the Samsung Health Monitor application.

- Then, press "**ECG**."
- Thereafter, choose "**Get Started**."
- Press the wrist you're putting on your smartwatch - Right or Left.
- After that, choose "**Done**." Your ECG information will be displayed.

Measure Blood Pressure

- Begin by swiping to the left on your smartwatch's main screen until you arrive at the Blood Pressure tile.
- Right there, press "**Learn More**."
- After that, choose "**Allow**."
- Next up, press "**Open phone app**." At this point, you'll be taken to the Samsung Health Monitor application on your smartphone, and hit on "**Calibrate the watch**."
- After that, press "**Next**."
- Thereafter, choose "**Get Started**."
- At this point, ensure you're putting on your Galaxy Watch on your wrist. Also, ensure the blood pressure monitor cuff is fitted on the arm where you're not putting on the smartwatch, although wearing the blood pressure monitor cuff is optional.
- Then, choose "**Next**."

- Start the blood pressure monitor, then wait to allow your Galaxy Watch to commence your blood pressure tracking.
- Next up, choose "**Yes, enter now**."
- Proceed by inserting the diastolic and systolic digits that show up on the blood pressure monitor.
- After the calibration is over, press "**OK**."

After the calibration is over, proceed to track your blood pressure directly on your smartwatch. The menu should display on your watch. However, if nothing appears, do this:

- Press the home button on your smartwatch to load the app list.
- Press the Samsung Health Monitor app.
- Next up, press "**Blood Pressure**."
- Then, press "**Measure**."
- Now, choose "**OK**." At this moment, the tracking will begin. After it's over, it'll show the analysis.

Measure your SpO2

Blood Oxygen tracking is also possible with your Galaxy smartwatch.

Adding the Blood Oxygen Tile

- Begin by swiping to the left on your watch's main screen to see the Blood Oxygen tile. However, if it's not there, press "**Add Tile**."
- Move to "**Blood Oxygen**."
- Thereafter, press the Blood Oxygen tile to add it to your Galaxy Watch.

Track Blood Oxygen

- Begin by swiping to the left on your watch's main screen to see the Blood Oxygen tile.
- Next up, choose "**Measure**."
- Proceed by swiping across the displayed guide.
- Then, press "**OK**."

Enable Blood Oxygen Tracking during Sleep

- Press the home button on your smartwatch to bring up the app list.
- Press the Samsung Health app.
- Move down, then press "**Settings**."
- Next up, press "**Measurements**."
- Thereafter, press "**Blood Oxygen During Sleep**."
- Go ahead and toggle turning on "**Measure Constantly**."

Track Floors Count

With your smartwatch, you can also monitor the number of floors you stroll each day.

- Navigate to your app list, then choose Samsung Health.
- Move down, then choose "**Floors**."
- From here, you'll be able to see an illustration of the number of floors you've walked.

In order to add floors target, do this:

- Navigate to your app list, then choose Samsung Health.
- Move down, then choose "**Floors**."
- Press "**More options**."
- Now, press "**Settings**."
- After which, choose "**Floor target**."
- Proceed by setting the target.
- Then, choose "**Done**."

Track Caffeine Intake

- Navigate to your app list, then choose Samsung Health.
- Move down, then choose "**Caffeine**."

- Hit on "**Add**" whenever you take a caffeinated drink.
- To delete an incorrect input, choose "**Remove**."

Chapter Ten

Make and Answer Calls

To ensure you can make and receive calls on your smartwatch, have the watch fastened to your wrist, and also ensure that both your smartwatch and phone are linked via a mobile network or Bluetooth.

With the LTE version of the Galaxy smartwatch, you'll be able to make and receive calls independently from your cell phone. If not, then you'll need your smartphone.

- Press the home button on the side of the smartwatch to see the application menu.
- Press the Phone app.
- Hit on the keypad icon to insert the number. Otherwise, press the contact icon to select a specific contact.
- Thereafter, press the green phone icon to make a call. At this stage, your linked smartphone will dial the call, and then your watch's speaker will act as the phone except if you are using a headphone.
- If you need to move the call from your smartwatch to your smartphone, long-tap the three dots on the display, then press "**Switch to phone**."

Answer Calls

Once you see an incoming call, swipe the phone icon toward the right of the watch's display to answer it. To decline, drag the red phone icon towards the left.

Once you're on a call and another call comes in, drag the green phone icon, then press and touch "**End current call**" to terminate the current call and answer it, or "**Hold current call**" to hold the current call. To return after you've held the initial call, press the triple vertical dots, then choose "**Swap**."

Sending a Text Message

- Press the home button on the side of the smartwatch to see the application menu.
- Press the Messages app.
- Thereafter, press the blue write button.
- Go ahead and insert the contact's name to locate it, or press the contacts button to pick from the list.
- Now, press "**Next**."
- Proceed by writing your message.
- Thereafter, press the send icon to submit the message.

How to use Quick Messages

- Head to the Galaxy Wearable application on your smartphone.
- In there, press "**Watch settings**."
- After which, press "**General**."
- Then, press "**Quick responses**."
- Swipe and press "+ **Add response**" to insert a new quick message.
- Proceed by filling in your desired text, then press "**Save**."
- If you'd rather edit an existing reply, press it, then fill in your desired text.
- Thereafter, press "**Save**."

Remove Messages

- Move to the Galaxy Wearable application on your smartphone.
- Then, press the Messages app.
- Move to the message you intend to erase.
- Long-tap on the message.
- After that, press "**Delete**."
- Then, press ✓.

Block Message Alerts

If you're bored with your watch sending message notifications, you can deactivate the alert.

- Move to the Galaxy Wearable application on your smartphone.
- Right there, press "**Watch settings**."
- Now, press "**Notifications**."
- Press the switch beside the Messages app to deactivate the message notification.

Block Messages

You can block someone in order to not see a message they have sent. You'll still get their message, but it'll only be seen under the blocked numbers menu and messages app.

- On your connected smartphone, navigate to the Messages app.
- Press the triple vertical dots.
- Now, press "**Settings**."
- Thereafter, press "**Block numbers and messages**."
- Right there, choose "**Block numbers**."
- Go ahead and insert the phone number.
- After which, press the green plus icon.

Enable SOS

Once you have SOS enabled, all you need to do during emergencies is press triple times on your watch's home button so that your watch will alert your saved emergency contact to your situation.

- Move to the Galaxy Wearable application on your connected smartphone.
- In there, press "**Watch Settings**."
- Thereafter select "**Advanced features**."
- After that, tap "**SOS**."
- Thereafter, hit on the "**When Home key is pressed three times**" switch to enable it or toggle on "**When hard fall detected**."
- Thereafter, press "**Continue**."
- After which, select "**Agree**."
- Go ahead and choose your desired Add emergency contact option.
- Hit on your desired contacts, then press "**Done**."
- Thereafter, tap **Save**.
- So, during emergencies, simply press the home button three times to alert your emergency contacts.

Chapter Eleven

Use the Samsung Flow App

With the Samsung Flow application, users can unlock their encrypted PC, smartphone, and even tablet by using the Galaxy smartwatch. This indicates that users don't need to fill in their password or enter their biometric data to unlock their devices.

However, you'll need to install the Samsung Flow application on your PC and smartphone for this to work.

Connecting Devices via Bluetooth

Ensure you have your smartwatch and PC or smartphone connected via Bluetooth.

Ensure you have a screen lock enabled on your watch and smartphone or PC.

- Press the home button on the side of the smartwatch to see the application menu.
- Press the Samsung Flow app.

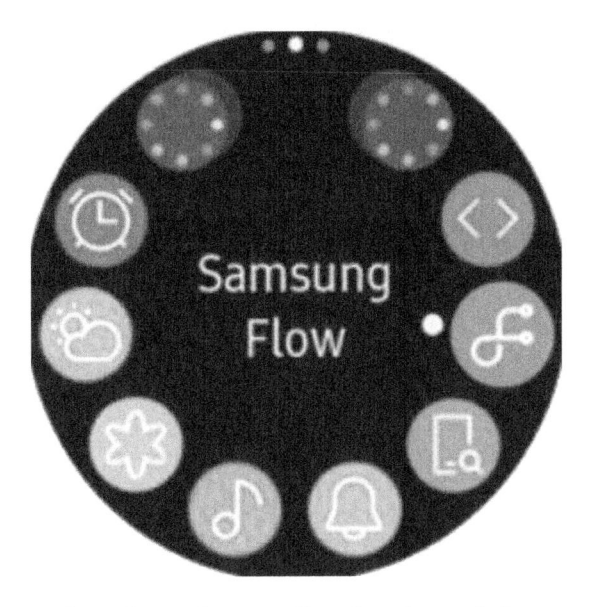

- After that, choose the checkmark icon.
- Thereafter, the watch will switch to Bluetooth pairing mode. At this point, your computer or smartphone will begin searching for your Watch.

Unlock the Computer/Tablet

- Take your watch close to the computer or smartphone.
- Proceed by turning the bezel clockwise to unlock the smartphone or PC.

Unlock your Computer/Tablet with Simple Unlock

- Press the home button on the side of the smartwatch to see the application menu.

- Press the Samsung Flow app.
- Thereafter, press the "**Simple unlock**" switch to activate it.
- Take your watch close to the computer or smartphone to automatically unlock it.

Manage PowerPoint Presentations with Watch

The Galaxy smartwatch can be used as a prop for PowerPoint presentations by navigating the slides, adding reminders to round off the presentation, etc.

Manage the Slides
- Press the home button on the side of the smartwatch to see the application menu.
- Press the PPT Controller app.
- In there, press "**Connect**."
- Head to the Bluetooth menu on your PC. Proceed by adding your watch as a Bluetooth device. You'll now be able to use the smartwatch to manage your slides.
- Move to the PowerPoint presentation on your PC.
- Press "**SLIDESHOW**" on your watch.

- Press the left or right arrow icons to load the next or previous slides.
- Press "**TOUCHPAD**" to also manage your PC's cursor through the smartwatch.

Enable Presentation Alerts

Interval alerts let you add reminders when to move to the next slides, while Wrap-up alerts enable you to set notifications when you need to finish the presentation.

- Press the home button on the side of the smartwatch to see the application menu.
- Press the PPT Controller app.
- Thereafter, press "**More options**."
- After which, press "**Wrap-up alert**" or "**Interval alerts**."

- Go ahead and choose our desired options.

Chapter Twelve

Import Music to the Watch

To play music from your Galaxy Watch, you must first have the music downloaded to your smartphone so that you can then export it to your watch.

- Move to the Galaxy Wearable application on your smartphone.
- Right there, press "**Watch Settings**."
- Move down, then press "**Manage content**."
- Thereafter, press "**Add tracks**."
- Go ahead and choose your desired songs.
- Then, choose "**Done**."
- Your selected songs will be transferred to your smartwatch. When everything is done, you'll get a notification.
- Thereafter, launch the Music Player application on your Galaxy Watch to access and listen to the tracks.

Remove Imported Music

- Head to the application list on your smartwatch.
- Then, choose the Music app.

- Move down, then select "**Library**."
- Hit on "**Tracks**."
- Locate the tracks you desire to delete. Long-tap on it, then choose "**Delete**."

Set up Vibration

The length and strength of vibration alerts can be customized to your preference.

- Press the home button of your Galaxy smartwatch to load the app list.
- Select the Settings app.
- Hit on "**Sounds and vibration**."
- Thereafter, choose "**Vibration**."
- Move to the "**Vibration intensity**" section to adjust the volume of the alerts.
- Head to the "**Vibration duration**" section to adjust the duration the alerts will vibrate.

Enable Call Vibration

You can make the vibration for incoming calls unique.

- Press the home button of your Galaxy smartwatch to load the app list.
- Select the Settings app.
- Thereafter, choose "**Sounds and vibration**."
- Next up, press "**Call vibration**."
- Go ahead and choose your desired vibration pattern.

Notification Vibration

- Press the home button of your Galaxy smartwatch to load the app list.
- Right there, choose the Settings app.
- Thereafter, choose "**Sounds and vibration**."
- After which, select "**Notification vibration**."
- Go ahead and choose your desired vibration pattern.

Set Watch Volume

- Press the home button of your Galaxy smartwatch to load the app list.
- Right there, choose the Settings app.
- Now, press "**Sounds and vibration**."

- Thereafter, press "**Volume**."
- Hit on a mode to adjust the volume.

Add Ringtone

- Press the home button of your Galaxy smartwatch to load the app list.
- Right there, choose the Settings app.
- Now, press "**Sounds and vibration**."
- Thereafter, press "**Ringtone**."
- Next up, choose a ringtone from the displayed list.

Add Notification Sound

- Press the home button of your Galaxy smartwatch to load the app list.
- Thereafter, choose the Settings app.
- Next up, select "**Sounds and vibration**."
- Right there, press "**Notification sound**."
- Press a notification sound to hear it play, then choose it.

Conclusion

Welcome to the end of the book. I'm sure you can now use and operate your Galaxy Watch the way you would love to. I hope this manual is able to make you know more about your Galaxy smartwatch and how it optimizes your healthy living and fitness goals.

Congrats!

About the Author

Shawn Blaine is a gadget reviewer, programmer, and computer geek. He has worked for some big tech companies in the past. He's currently focused on coding and blockchain development but still finds time to write and teach people how to use their smart devices to the fullest.

Other Books by the Author

- Amazon Echo Dot 5th Generation User Guide

https://amzn.to/40pJbC5

- Amazon Kindle 11th Generation User Guide

https://amzn.to/3HVRBK0

- iPad Pro 2022 User Guide

https://amzn.to/3l8xvUh

- iPad 10th Generation User Guide

https://amzn.to/3X5pSLk

- iPhone 14 Pro Max User Guide

https://amzn.to/3X6vEfM

- Kindle Fire HD 8 & HD 8 Plus (2022) User Guide

https://amzn.to/3DCWLbg

- Samsung Galaxy S23 Ultra 5G User Guide

https://amzn.to/43KQuFB

- Samsung Galaxy S23 User Guide

https://amzn.to/3PhUOIf

Index

A

Accessibility Shortcut 83
Add Notification Sound 132
Add Ringtone.... 132
Add Screen Lock. 28
Airplane Mode 25
Alarm 90, 91
Alerts.... 50, 52, 122, 127
Always on Display 20
Automatic Workout Detection 95

B

Back up Galaxy Watch 11
Bedtime Mode 56
Bixby 41, 42, 44, 47, 60
Block Messages. 122
Bluetooth 22, 23, 24, 25, 119, 124, 125, 126

C

Camera Controller 79
Change Brightness 18
Charge the Galaxy Watch 8
Clear Storage 20
Continuous Heart Rate 94
Customize Hearing 82

D

Disable Coaching Messages 110
Disconnection Alerts 22
Do Not Disturb .. 59, 60
Double Press Key 83

E

Enable SOS 123

F

Fall Detection 98
Floors Count 117

136

G

Gallery App 79
Google Assistant 42, 43, 44, 46, 47, 60
Google Maps 76

H

Heart Rate 94, 95
Home Key Settings 47

I

Import Music to the Watch 129
Install Apps 65

K

Keyboard Input Language 62

M

Make and Answer Calls 119
Manage Apps Data 68
Measure Blood Pressure 114
Measure ECG 111
Measure Heart Rate Manually 94
Measure Stress ... 99
Measure your SpO2 115

Mobile Networks . 16
Monitor Woman's Health 103

N

NFC 89, 90
Notification Vibration 131

P

Power Saving Mode 26
PowerPoint Presentations . 126

Q

Quick Messages . 121

R

Remove Messages 121
Reset your Galaxy Watch 14

S

Samsung Flow App 124
Samsung Pay 85, 88, 89
Screen Timeout ... 19
Set the Time and Date 63
Set up Vibration 130

Set up Workout ... 93
Set Watch Volume 131
Sleep Coaching 1, 97, 98
Snore Detection .. 96
Stopwatch 91

T

TalkBack 81, 82
Text Message 120
Theater Mode 58
Timer 92
Track Caffeine Intake 117
Track your Body Composition .. 107
Track your Steps 100
Turn on Watch 8

U

Uninstall Apps 67

Update Watch Apps 75
Update your Watch Software 74

V

Visibility Enhancements . 81
Voice Assistant Language 60
Voice Commands 41
Voice Input Language 61

W

Watch Faces 29
Water Lock ... 53, 54
Wi-Fi 23
Wireless PowerShare . 9, 10
Wrist Orientation 21

Printed in Great Britain
by Amazon